WAYPOINTS

Tools and Tactics for Life's Toughest Choices

MATT MILLER

WAYPOINTS: Tools and Tactics for Life's Toughest Choices

© 2025 by Matt Miller

PUBLISHED BY MOKOM PRESS

ISBN: 979-8-9992105-1-7

Printed in the United States of America

PRAISE FOR WAYPOINTS

"Waypoints offers something we badly need more of: practical wisdom for making better choices. Matt is helping people think for themselves, and that's a public service."

—Andrew Yang
Entrepreneur, Author, Co-Chair of the Forward Party, 2020 Presidential Candidate

"Miller brings a seasoned perspective to a landscape that many advisors and consultants meet with only a jaded eye. With empathy for how we use our limited resources—in wealth, time, and attention—to make meaning, Matt Miller meets readers where they are in a time when so many decisions compete for our focus. In a trustworthy, forthright style, he offers guidance to help readers align actions with values, empower confident decisions, and create something more: lasting, lifelong satisfaction."

—Margot Bloomstein
Speaker, Consultant, and Author of Trustworthy

"Waypoints isn't just about making better decisions—it's about getting started on the right foot or regaining control in a world that constantly pushes us off course. Matt Miller blends behavioral insight, lived experience, and hard-won wisdom into a guide that's deeply personal yet widely applicable. Part memoir, part decision-making manual, this is a practical toolkit for life's pivotal choices."

—John D. Anderson
Thought Leader, Speaker, and Practice Management Expert

"Matt's unique, and much-needed, contribution to decision-making is an approach that engages both heart and mind, without sacrificing either. In Waypoints, he explores common big life decisions with thoughtful, reflective insights on how to stay true to yourself and your values. He alternates between life decision chapters and accessible, practical guidance on the decision-making process itself, including clear tools and tips you can use. This book is a valuable companion for anyone facing major choices or simply seeking to make smarter decisions that feel more authentic."

—Jane Macy, PhD
Faculty, University of Washington School of Social Work (Retired)

"What we decide—and how we decide—are among the most consequential things we do as humans. Understanding what information matters, knowing where you stand, making decisions, and taking timely action is key to success. In Waypoints, Matt Miller takes us on a thoughtful, insightful journey into the decision-making process. He offers a practical framework for both understanding how we make choices and improving the quality of those choices in real life."

—Brian Smith
Chief of Police, Port Angeles Police Department

"Matt Miller makes complex ideas feel approachable and understandable. His use of real-world examples makes this a valuable resource for professionals and everyday readers alike."

—Wendy Sisk
CEO, Peninsula Behavioral Health

"Waypoints offers timeless wisdom for making better decisions at every stage of life. As someone in the later chapters of my own journey, I believed I already understood my decision-making processes, but Waypoints sharpened that understanding and added new depth. Thank you, Matt."

—Bob Podrat, MA, MBA
Executive Coach and Consultant

TABLE OF CONTENTS

INTRODUCTION

I grew up in a rare "sweet spot" in history, after the era of duck-and-cover atomic bomb drills, but before the age of active shooter lockdowns. Call it perfect timing. I count myself lucky never to have lost a close friend or family member to terrorism or war. Sadly though, fewer people can say the same today.

In the fall of 2012, I was in Denver with Amy, now my wife, who was visiting from New York. We were enjoying a leisurely downtown stroll when an unsettling feeling washed over me. I couldn't shake the feeling that something was wrong. In his book Blink, Malcolm Gladwell might describe this phenomenon as "thin-slicing," relying on subtle cues or patterns that our unconscious mind detects, even when we're not consciously aware of them.

Gladwell explains, "There are moments, particularly in times of stress, when haste does not make waste, when our snap judgments and first impressions can offer a much better means of making sense of the world." This felt like one of those moments.

As I scanned the public square, I noticed something strange: instead of the usual purposeful flow of pedestrians, people instead seemed to mill about without direction. I focused on a group of people in their twenties who appeared to be waiting for something. They were spaced out around the square, exchanging nervous glances and trying to act inconspicuously. Fearing the worst, I told Amy that we needed to leave.

She wanted to stay and see what was happening. As we debated, the suspicious individuals slowly converged on the square while oblivious pedestrians walked through their shrinking circle. Taking hold of Amy's elbow, I attempted to pull her away from the potential harm. She reluctantly followed me across the street. And then it happened.

On that otherwise ordinary autumn day, Writer Square in Denver suddenly burst into song! The "suspicious conspirators" were actually a flash mob, bursting into a musical number from The Rocky Horror Picture Show. College-aged entertainers danced and sang their hearts out, delighting everyone lucky enough to witness it. Amy, ever the musical theater superfan, was overwhelmed with glee and even shed a few happy tears. The flash mob became a highlight of her trip and a memory we still cherish.

Reflecting on that experience, I feel a mix of emotions. I recall the anxiety of wanting to escape and the simultaneous frustration of trying to convince someone I cared about of a perceived danger. I feel proud for recognizing what I thought was danger, even if it wasn't. But I also cringe at the memory of pulling her away seconds before the show began. Sometimes I worry that Amy's curiosity, so often a source of joy, might one day put her in danger. The cautious part of me says it's better to miss a thousand flash mobs than to be caught in a single tragedy. But my inner idealist wonders: if we trade joy for fear, haven't we already lost something magical?

What was the right decision on that day in Denver? Was my judgment influenced by a modern media landscape that disproportionately focuses on tragedies rather than moments of celebration? Should it matter that being wrong meant missing a performance, but being right might have meant avoiding tragedy? In hindsight, it wasn't life or death, but in that moment, we had no way to know that.

I give advice for a living. I tell hundreds of people each year: I don't have a crystal ball. And even if I did, most wouldn't listen. This book isn't for them.

In Greek mythology, Cassandra was cursed with prophecy. "Cursed?" you might ask. "Don't you mean gifted?" No. That word was chosen carefully. You see, Cassandra was granted the ability to see the future. Her fate? To deliver her prophecies, but never be believed.

As I said above, I can't see the future. But I do have a gift for seeing into the past. Okay, maybe it's not really a gift. It's called memory, and everyone has it. But I do have something rarer: pattern recognition. And sometimes, the line between that and prophecy is razor-thin and just as K follows HIJ, we can predict what follows a night of heavy drinking and the decision to drive yourself home. Try explaining that to a drunk person who is insisting that "I can drive," and you might start to understand why Cassandra's ability is now considered to have been a curse. What is the point of knowing that a disaster is coming if you can do nothing about it?

> "Learn from the mistakes of others. You can't live long enough to make them all yourself."
> —Eleanor Roosevelt

Many never learn from their own mistakes. Some learn from experience and do better. But the truly wise? They learn from others' mistakes. Touching a hot stove will hurt you. We all know this, and yet we all know someone who insists on learning the hard way. You can scream a warning. You can show your own scars. Still, they won't listen. This book isn't for them. It's for the ones who still have a shot at avoiding the burn. Few things frustrate me more than seeing someone about to make a bad decision knowing I can't change their mind. That's my own Cassandra's curse.

Since many won't heed a warning, I'll salve my conscience by helping those willing to listen and learn. Since I won't be there to slap your hand away from every hot stove, I want to give you tools to spot the danger, step back, and learn from other people's scars instead of your own.

Warren Buffett, long-serving CEO of Berkshire Hathaway, is one of the wealthiest individuals in the world. In an annual letter to shareholders, the legendary investor wrote that Berkshire Hathaway's exceptional performance was 'the product of about a dozen truly good decisions. That would be about one every five years.'

If it's true that just a handful of decisions shape our long-term success and happiness, then two things matter most: spotting those pivotal moments and getting them right. This book aims to help you achieve both.

After decades in personal finance, I've come to realize: I'm not just managing money. I'm helping people make decisions. I gather all the useful information I can about an individual or family, their resources, fears, experiences, and ambitions, and combine it with knowledge of the world, available tools, and likely outcomes.

An industry friend boils my profession down to "helping people make better decisions with their money," but over time, I have discovered that this is too narrow a scope. Good investment returns help, but they can't overcome the damage done by bad life decisions. It may be hard to be happy in a bad marriage and harder still to offset a 50% loss in net worth from divorce, no matter how smart your investments are. Likewise, investment gains pale in comparison to the income boost that comes from choosing the right career. Everyone's "dozen truly good decisions" will be different, but there are five or six that pop up rather frequently. These may be among the most important if your definition of success includes true contentment.

The chapters ahead explore specific decisions that can dramatically shape your life, from choosing a partner to managing your finances. You'll also find tools, strategies, and frameworks to tackle other decisions that might be part of your own 'big twelve.' These tools aren't just for the decisions I've identified; they're built to help you with the unpredictable, personal ones, too.

CHAPTER 1

HEROICS BE DAMNED:

SAVE YOUR SHIP.

"Choices are the hinges of destiny."
—*PYTHAGORAS*—

ONE POPULAR BUSINESS TROPE romanticizes the idea of going ashore and 'burning the ships.' The phrase traces back to 1519, when Spanish Captain Hernán Cortés landed in what is now Mexico with 600 men. (I put 'New World' in quotes intentionally; it was anything but new to the Aztecs who swam out to greet them.) When the Europeans arrived on land, Cortés gave the order to burn the ships, leaving stolen Aztec boats as their only way home. While the story has little else to offer, it exemplifies extreme commitment, hence its appeal to those who believe 'failure is not an option.'

For our purposes, it also illustrates the classical definition of a decision. The word "decide" derives its significance from the Latin term "decidere," formed by merging two words: *"de,"* meaning 'OFF,' and *"caedere,"* meaning 'CUT.' To decide is to **cut off other paths**; it's a commitment, not a trial run. In my view, that's about where the story's usefulness ends.

Unnecessarily burning one's boats is foolish at best. Especially when those boats might be your only way home. If failure was ever simply an "option," who would choose it? Being wrong isn't just a possibility; it's inevitable for anyone bold enough to take chances on an uncertain future.

I once spoke with a young man considering dropping out of high school. "I just want to live, man," he told me, passionately rejecting the idea that his dreams required formal education. His words, in their own way, echoed a universal desire: freedom without friction. Instead of challenging his mindset, I talked to him about how dropping out would be like abandoning a perfectly seaworthy ship without knowing if he could swim. While an educated person can later choose a simpler life, a dropout cannot simply choose one that requires a diploma. By deciding to quit school, they have cut off that potential future. There's nothing wrong with wanting to dive into life, but wise sailors don't sink their ship just to feel the splash.

While this book is about tactics and techniques for making decisions, it is not about eliminating options unnecessarily. In fact, I advise that you never "burn the ships" if there is no clear benefit to doing so. When problems arise, as they inevitably will, it is good to know that you have kept a "Plan B" intact.

LIVING TO FIGHT ANOTHER DAY

Maybe you don't have to act right away. Perhaps another decision takes precedence. Sometimes, there's no harm in waiting. Letting time pass can bring perspective and experience, both helpful when making a better-informed decision.

I'm no fan of bullfighting, but I do love a powerful metaphor. The matador is a perfect example of someone who benefits from *not* acting immediately. Consider the matador standing in the ring as he stares down a charging bull. He cannot run, or else he will certainly be caught and severely injured. He cannot fight a gigantic angry animal head to head, or he very well may not keep his own head attached to his neck. He must hold still. He must stay composed, waiting until just the right moment as the bull charges. He must confidently step aside at exactly the right moment to avoid the threat and let it charge past him unharmed. The reason is simple: the cost of failure is high, and the cost of waiting is only a little time. He can defeat the bull when the time is right, but only if he isn't already in a hospital bed when that time comes.

How can we apply this to the decisions that we may face? There are three lessons we should take from the matador.

1. **Do not panic**. Things are probably not moving as quickly as they first appear. It's okay to pause and breathe. Panicking may cause harm.
2. **Trust your ability to maneuver**. Your best move may be to sidestep, not charge. Waiting doesn't mean standing in harm's way.
3. **You don't have to win right now.** Your only job is to survive *this* charge. Winning comes later, but only if you're still standing.

How do you know when a decision can wait and when it can't? Meet the Eisenhower Matrix. This tool, also known as the "Eisenhower Box," is a simple tool you can use to prioritize the issues in front of you. It was popularized by Dwight D. Eisenhower, the 34th President of the United States, who was known for his ability to manage his time efficiently.

The matrix categorizes issues based on the answers to only two questions: "Is it urgent?" and "Is it important?" Decisions that are both urgent and important must come first. These demand immediate attention; ignoring them can come with real consequences. These could be emergencies or items with critical deadlines.

If a decision is important but not urgent, schedule time to address it; just don't put it off forever. These are probably long-term in nature but contribute to your goals, success, or life satisfaction. Be cautious about putting these off indefinitely, though, as the price you pay may be that they become urgent. Set aside a specific time to make these decisions. These may involve topics like long-term relationship building, business strategy, or planning personal activities.

Urgent but not important? Delegate it if you can. While you likely do not have White House Aides or a Presidential Cabinet to take on your less important decisions, perhaps you still have some people in your life who are simply better suited or more interested in handling them.

If something is neither urgent nor important, don't waste your time on it. Simply forget about issues like these.

The Eisenhower Matrix

	NOT URGENT	URGENT
IMPORTANT	SCHEDULE (Long-term strategic goals)	DO FIRST (Critical tasks with deadlines)
NOT IMPORTANT	ELIMINATE (Time-wasters, distractions)	DELEGATE (Tasks others can handle)

The process is simple. Just follow these four steps of using the Eisenhower Decision Matrix:

1. List the decisions you need to make.
2. Evaluate each situation to determine its level of urgency and importance.
3. Sort into four categories:
   a. Do First (Urgent and Important)
   b. Schedule for Later (Important but not Urgent)
   c. Delegate (Urgent but not Important)
   d. Avoid or Minimize (Not Urgent nor Important)
4. Act Accordingly

Now that you have some idea of what decisions to make and when to make them, we should talk about how to increase the odds of good results.

BEYOND THE POSSIBILITY OF DEFEAT

"The good fighters of old first put themselves beyond the possibility of defeat, and then waited for an opportunity of defeating the enemy."
— Sun Tzu

When my GPS gives an arrival time, I often take it as a personal challenge. On long road trips, making 'good time' becomes a kind of sport. Not that I drive recklessly (in case my insurer is reading), but I do treat the ETA as a time to beat. All that said, I still fasten my seatbelt before I even start the engine. Before chasing the best outcome, it makes sense to first guard against the worst one.

In my day job as a financial planner, this means helping families build the assets, strategies, and habits to survive anything life throws at them. They are essentially "beyond the possibility of defeat." Only once this has been achieved may we turn our attention to the search for outsized returns.

Defeat looks different for everyone. Maybe it's a physical injury, emotional heartbreak, or a financial crash like bankruptcy. You can't defend against defeat until you define what it looks like. This process is what German mathematician Carl Gustav Jacob might call *umkehren*, a term meaning to reverse, turn back, or invert. We might call it working backward from defeat.

Charlie Munger, billionaire investor and Vice Chairman of Berkshire Hathaway, once famously said, "All I want to know is where I'm going to die, so I'll never go there." If he knew what would cause his demise, he could avoid it by steering clear of the conditions that lead to it. This makes good sense. Let's consider a couple of examples where one could reverse engineer a bad outcome in order to avoid poor decisions.

Take bankruptcy, for example. If most bankruptcies involve unmanageable debt and no plan to repay it, that tells you something about how to approach borrowing or opening new credit card accounts. If you notice that many bankruptcies stem from excessive medical bills from injury or illness, it might make sense to double-check that you have adequate insurance coverage. By working backward from an undesirable result, you can create your own lists of hazards to avoid in your day-to-day decisions.

Later in this book, we will discuss choosing a partner in some detail. For now, let's reverse engineer a poor outcome for a marriage. Let's ask: What are the warning signs that tend to precede divorce? Over time, money problems have consistently contributed to divorce. Nearly half of American couples say they argue about money. Depending on the generation, 29% to 41% of divorcees cite money as the main reason for their split. This may be a good indication that a couple should prioritize some degree of financial security before getting married.

As with any success or failure, not all decisions are so grand in nature. There are usually a few "one-off" decisions that may correlate with a bad outcome. If we continue to use a failed marriage as an undesirable outcome, we can look at something as specific as the wedding itself. Two Emory University professors, Andrew Francis-Tan and Hugo M. Mialon, did a study in 2015 that showed a clear relationship between the duration of marriages and two very specific costs. Using data from over 3,000 married Americans, they found that couples who spent less on weddings and rings tended to stay married longer. Specifically, their work showed that wedding costs exceeding $20,000 led to divorce 1.6 times more often than those with a tab of between $5,000 and $10,000. Using our method of inverting a failure to increase the odds of success, an engaged couple might choose to "keep it simple" when it comes to the big party and the associated jewelry. If the evidence above isn't convincing enough, one group with a below-average divorce rate is couples that spent less than $1,000 tying the knot.

There is a saying that, "success leaves clues." So does failure. When we know what failure looks like, we can make the decisions that help us avoid it. When faced with a choice, do not take the option that will lead you into disaster.

MAKE YOUR DESIRED OUTCOME
INEVITABLE

While we're still talking about romance, let me confess to ruining a perfectly good love story. Now, let me be clear about a couple of things. Firstly, I am as big of a romantic as the next guy, more so, perhaps. Secondly, this was a casual night out, over cocktails, with some close friends, not a wedding reception, so when a friend exclaimed, "It was a miracle!" "How else can you explain that I would just happen to be on a flight seated next to the man who was meant to be my husband?" I went ahead and burst her bubble. "It's just math," I explained. This was met with silence and raised eyebrows.

Let's say you are walking down the sidewalk and see a building with a line of people stretched around the block. The line snakes its way into a small building and out a separate door. It looks to take about 10-20 seconds for a person to make it from the entrance to the exit. The line is moving pretty quickly, so you get in to see what the fuss is about. When you enter the building, you see a man at a table. He flips a coin. It comes up heads. He flips it again. Heads again. Before the natural pace of the line moves you back out onto the sidewalk, you witness the man flip the coin ten times, and it lands on heads every time! Clearly, this is some sort of wizardry! Or is it?

The odds of flipping an "honest" coin to land on heads ten times in a row on your first attempt is 1 in 1024. Let me first state that most people would assume this to be a far less likely outcome than that. In this example, however, there are other very important details that I left out. We don't know how many other people saw ten heads come up. We don't know if anyone else in that line witnessed a similar outcome. Another thing we don't know is how long this man has been sitting there flipping that coin. Mathematically, if he was doing it for six hours or more, it is likely that at least a couple of people witnessed ten heads in a row. Given enough time, that eventual outcome is not an anomaly at all, but rather it is inevitable. (For more on this math, you can look at: https://nrich.maths.org/problems/derren-brown-coin-flipping-scam?tab=solutions).

Let's get back to my friend on the plane. We will start with the large numbers. In 2017, at any given moment, one could confirm that there was an average of 9,728 passenger planes in the air carrying 1,270,406 people. Considering the number of potential mates in the air, it seems inevitable that a few of them would strike up a conversation and hit it off! In this case, there were even several factors that increased the odds. For starters, they were in the tiny minority of the human population that could afford air travel. Furthermore, it turns out that they were passengers on a weekday flight between New York City and San Francisco. Any experienced traveler will tell you that certain flights lend themselves to business travel, and this was one of them. This increases the odds that your neighbor will be of working age, in a certain income bracket, and traveling alone. As if this wasn't a good enough set-up for a mid-air love connection, they were seated in business class! This narrows down the demographics of the travelers even further and adds some free alcohol to keep the conversation going! By the time I had completed my analysis, my poor friend's "how we met" miracle seemed almost inevitable. At one point, I found myself wondering why dating services weren't just booking singles on flights every day!

Here's the thing: I concede that it wasn't exactly a "sure thing" that my friend would be seated next to "Mr. Right" on that plane. As we determined, however, several factors at play made the outcome more likely, and therein lies the lesson.

We can't control outcomes. Not entirely. Luck and randomness always play a role. What we can do every day is increase the odds of the outcomes we want. Like that couple in business class, we can stack the odds in our favor with good timing and smart positioning. We must be willing to take advantage of such opportunities and take precautions to avoid potential mishaps. Let's not forget that if you are not seated next to the right neighbor today, there is always another flight waiting to take off. Combine smart strategies with enough opportunities, and your "miracle" becomes a matter of math. Your success might almost seem inevitable.

TOOLS FOR YOUR KIT

KEY INSIGHT: Success isn't just about what you pursue; it's also about what you protect. Resilience comes from building wisely, retreating strategically, and preparing for both victory and defeat.

MENTAL REFRAME: Sometimes the bravest move isn't all-in; it's being smart enough to keep an exit plan. Avoid romanticizing "burn the boats" if the shore you're landing on might change.

PRACTICAL TOOL: Use the Eisenhower Matrix (*p.11*) to sort your actions into what's urgent and important, versus what can wait or be dropped entirely. It's not about doing more; it's about doing what matters most now.

ACTION STEP: Sketch out your current challenge in four boxes:

1. Urgent & Important
2. Important but Not Urgent
3. Urgent but Not Important
4. Neither Urgent nor Important

Then move one item from the 'urgent but not important' box to the trash.

BONUS TOOL: Before chasing a goal, define your worst-case scenario. What guardrails can you put in place now to make sure you can recover, even if things go wrong? That's how you engineer your own "miracle."

CHAPTER 2

CHOOSING A PARTNER:

WHO'S IN YOUR CORNER

THE SUMMER OF 2018 HIT HARD. I had to swallow a bitter pill: I'd made a major mistake. I walked away from a business I had poured years of time and energy into. On my attorney's advice, I left behind hundreds of thousands in equity. There were plenty of small issues, but one big decision caused them all: I chose a terrible partner. The partnership was failing because he was greedy and dishonest. I walked away because he was notoriously litigious, with the resources to drag things out in court. I didn't have that luxury.

A few years earlier, Amy and I left Colorado, a place I could have happily called home for life. We sold our beautiful house, and I resigned from a lucrative job in order to "settle down" and buy into the practice of a retiring professional. We made an immediate payment of $50,000 and wrote several more checks every few months as we worked through our written succession plan. After all that sacrifice, I had to explain to my wife that it had all been for nothing. She was upset, but never at me. Her compassion and confidence guided us through the question: 'Where do we go from here?' It wasn't easy, but it could've been so much worse. Why wasn't it? Because I'd chosen a wonderful partner!

Oprah Winfrey once instructed her audience to "Surround yourself only with people who are going to take you higher." This concept affects everything, your happiness, career, even your health. My story shows both sides of the partnering coin, the good and the disastrous. Business partners and romantic partners aren't the same, but the tools for choosing them well often are.

ONE IMPORTANT ASSUMPTION
TO QUESTION

When facing a tough decision, always step back and examine your assumptions. For instance, the very existence of this chapter suggests that partnering up is inevitable. Let me be clear: you may not need a partner. In business, in life or even in tennis. For instance, marriage may not be the right choice for everyone. Going back to the previous chapter, one might also question whether or not it is simply the right time to partner up. If not, it may be a good idea to wait. You don't owe the world a partner. Make that call on your own terms.

Letting internal principles, not external pressure, guide your decisions is key to a tool I've developed. This is a simple method for exploring your options through the lens of your own internal mechanisms.

"MAKING" A PARTNERSHIP

In his book, *Maybe (Maybe Not)*, author Robert Fulghum describes a scene where a couple from the Isle of Crete was overheard arguing, and other Cretans smiled saying, "Ah, they are making love." Needless to say, as a native English speaker, the author had an entirely different understanding of the term "making love." Fulghum's point is that building a partnership is an ongoing process and not always a pretty one.

That story hit home for me, twice. First, it reminded me of my parents' marriage, which lasted for several decades, "until death did they part". I saw that keeping a marriage strong involved a daily effort to bridge the natural gap between two people with different perspectives. It took countless tiny gestures, an abundance of patience, some swallowing of pride, and biting of tongues. I can't say for certain that they woke up each morning "in love," but I can confidently say that they "made" their love every day.

It also reminded me of how we often romanticize professional partnerships when they, too, require daily work. It occurs to me that many people have the same unrealistic notion of business partnerships that others may have of love. Signing a contract doesn't make you partners; doing the work does. The concept of true partnership should be more like the idea of love on the Island of Crete.

Partners should expect to do the work of "making" their alliance every day. This is a long commitment to humility and patience. It is understanding that there is always more to learn and that the world and its inhabitants will not stop changing, even if you wish they would. While time and experience are part of the equation, a lifetime of simply calling oneself a partner will compare poorly to the results of fewer years spent engaging in the work of building a partnership.

THE PROBLEM WITH OPTIONS

One common reason partnerships fail? Lack of true commitment. Especially if they believe there are "plenty of fish in the sea." After all, why work so hard when there is a seemingly infinite supply of potential partners waiting for you?

In his 2004 book, *The Paradox of Choice: Why More is Less*, psychologist Barry Schwartz introduced me to the term "Tyranny of Choice." This is the suggestion that an abundance of options can be overwhelming to the point of resulting in an almost predictable sense of dissatisfaction. With so many options, some people constantly worry they didn't choose 'the best' partner. Taken to its extremes, this could lead to a never-ending sense of regret and unhappiness. Some studies have found that true contentment with one's decisions may not come from choosing the best option but rather from one's level of confidence in having done so. Sometimes, a smaller dating pool is a blessing, not a curse. After all, your odds of picking the "right" one from a group of ten are much better than from a group of ten million.

It is for this reason that our better-connected and therefore shrinking world may be working against anyone's odds of being content with their choice of partner. With tens of millions on dating apps, it's easy to believe your perfect match is just one swipe away.

In a 2000 study by psychologists Sheena Iyenger and Mark Lepper (from Columbia and Stanford, respectively), a simple experiment shed light on the downside of having too many choices. On different days in a grocery store, the team set up two display tables with a variety of jams. Stopping by to sample some jams earned the shopper a $1 off coupon for any of the products. There was only one difference between the two displays. One had six types of jam to choose from, and the other had 24.

The common belief in today's society is that having more choices is inherently better. Believing this, it wouldn't have been much of a surprise that the larger display gathered more visitors than the smaller one.

This is where advantages stopped, however. Using the coupons as a way to measure actual product sales, it turned out that visitors to the smaller table were ten times more likely to eventually make a purchase! Studies like this one have gone on to prove that being overwhelmed with choice not only decreases the chances that someone will make a decision at all but also decreases their eventual satisfaction with the decision that they made.

Getting back to the topic of searching for a partner, let's consider the opposite of an infinite supply of potential romantic mates. Rather than the world of dating apps, we can consider an arranged marriage. I can't think of a smaller "dating pool" than the one that contains a single predetermined mate. Putting aside cultural differences for a moment, one can't help but notice the numbers. In 2022, the divorce rate for arranged marriages was astonishingly less than one-tenth that of the rate for U.S. marriages as a whole.

This type of statistic holds up if we widen the opportunity set up a bit farther than just one potential mate. Historically, U.S. divorce rates were significantly lower when a person's choices were limited to the people in their social circle or their immediate geographic area. The rates increased through most of the 20th century as people became more mobile and their pool of potential mates expanded.

Understanding the "Tyranny of Choice," we might ask ourselves how we can reduce the vast universe of potential partners down to a shortlist to increase our chances of long-term happiness and satisfaction. I suggest that we start with the concept of approaching a problem from the inside out. In the paragraphs below, I offer you a simple and memorable system for making several life decisions, from choosing a career path to deciding where to live. For now, let's break it in with the decision to choose a life partner.

THE PRISM PROTOCOL

I have discovered that there are three levels of criteria that one can consider when making complex personal decisions. They differ in the depth of their personal importance. This is what I call inside-out decision-making. The trick that I suggest for remembering the tool is the term "PRism Protocol." The first consideration in this process is Principles, followed by Priorities, and lastly Preferences. While this is a very versatile method, let's apply it now to the specific process of choosing a romantic partner or spouse.

The PRism Protocol
(Inside-Out Decision Making)

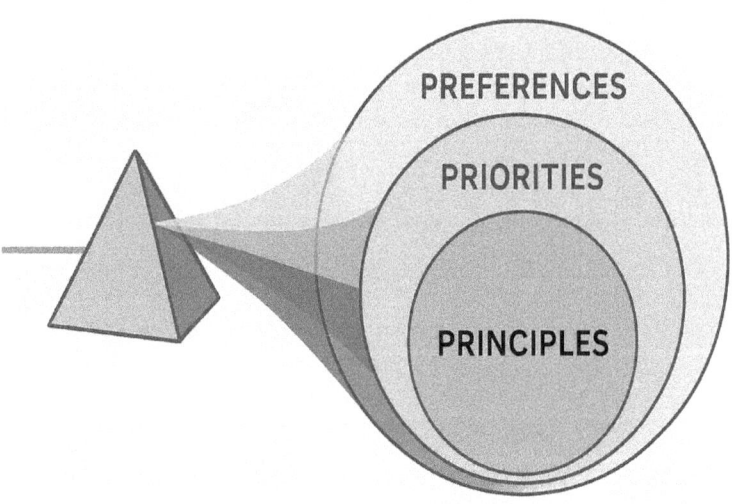

Principles

Your personal values should stand as the foundation of your decision-making process. These are your core beliefs about what is right and wrong and include your sense of justice and personhood. They do vary from person to person and can also evolve over time. When choosing a romantic partner, one might look for evidence of personal principles like compassion and loyalty. Your list might include components of religious doctrine or something like a shared sense of environmental consciousness. While your principles may be shaped by your upbringing, experiences, philosophy, or religion, it could also be something much more simple. One common principle that supported my own decision to marry was a common understanding of how people should treat each other.

If you both hold the same things sacred across all environments, you've found solid ground on which to potentially build a partnership.

Priorities

My wife and I love to travel. Every now and then, we find ourselves in a conversation about a foreign country we've visited or a unique cultural experience that we enjoyed in an exotic locale. Frequently, someone will say, "You two are so lucky!" We usually just share a quick look at one another and exchange knowing smiles. Inside, we know the truth. Yes. We are undoubtedly very fortunate people for countless reasons. Our well-worn passports are a direct result of our priorities. A combination of our principles and priorities led us to the decision to not have children. This grants us a great deal of freedom (and certainly some extra spending cash). We don't drive expensive cars or subscribe to every available streaming service. We might like these things, but they are not a higher priority than our desire to see the world together.

Once you have determined that your core principles align with a possible partner, you can consider whether or not your priorities are compatible. These priorities may include your life goals and aspirations. These may, in turn, overlap with conversations about each of your career ambitions. As in the example above, conversations around your thoughts about parenting or caring for other family members may be useful in discussing priorities.

Patient, open, and respectful conversation is a must when working to understand someone's priorities. Ensuring that theirs do not conflict with yours is key to building a lasting partnership.

Preferences

"My wife and I don't compete. We know each other's preferences, and we work to provide those for each other. One will take over when the other is faced with something he or she dislikes. That's what friends do."
—Matthew McConaughey

I recall a conversation when I was listing the desirable features of an ideal romantic partner to a close friend. I was single, and we were in our young twenties. The details on my list had to do with whether she could snowboard, play volleyball, or how often she could beat me in a chess match. Not too long after this conversation, I introduced him to a lovely woman whom I had seen a couple of times. She was a terrific person in many ways but not a chess player. In a quiet moment after they met, my buddy said to me, "You can just let her win a game." My close friend understood, better than I did, the difference between my priorities and my mere preferences.

I would prefer it if Amy enjoyed foreign-language films. She does not. Our mutual enjoyment of movie nights is a priority, so I watch the subtitled ones on my own time. I imagine she would prefer it if I deeply enjoyed the process of shopping for purses. She goes to those stores alone. The nature of the preference level of this system is that you shouldn't expect to get everything you would prefer. You should appreciate the wins (we both love dogs!) and be willing to communicate and negotiate around the rest ("You give them a bath. I'll clean up the yard.").

If you asked me 25 years ago to write a list of attributes for my future wife, then traveled in time so I could read it today, I would very likely be in tears from how hard I would laugh at my younger self. Almost every feature I thought was important back then has been tossed aside in the years since. Many of them were discarded when I met my future wife. I was a fool to have built a wife-shaped box into which someone would have to fit. Thankfully, I met someone who didn't need to fit the mold, because she reshaped it.

TOOLS FOR YOUR KIT

CHOOSING A PARTNER

KEY INSIGHT: The question isn't just who to choose, but why, when, and whether a partnership is right for you at all. Clarity comes from alignment, not just attraction.

MENTAL REFRAME: You're not looking for someone to complete you; you're looking for someone to complement a life you're already proud of.

PRACTICAL TOOL: Use the PRism Protocol to sort your criteria:

- **Principles:** Non-negotiables rooted in your values (e.g., honesty, growth, kindness).
- **Priorities:** Lifestyle goals and routines (e.g., kids, career ambition, health).
- **Preferences:** Flexible bonuses (e.g., music taste, height, style).

This inside-out approach helps you stay grounded when emotions or chemistry cloud your judgment.

ACTION STEP: List 3 personal principles, 3 life priorities, and 3 preferences. Use this list as a compass, not a checklist, when evaluating future or current partners.

BONUS TOOL: Be mindful of choice fatigue. Dating apps and endless profiles can trick you into believing that better is always one swipe away. Fewer, more intentional choices often lead to greater fulfillment.

CHAPTER 3

BIAS:

YOUR BRAIN COULD
BE LYING TO YOU

ANCHORING IS WHEN YOUR BRAIN CLINGS to irrelevant information as a reference point for new decisions. It's one of the most common cognitive biases, where irrelevant reference points are used to shape new choices.

I started playing competitive volleyball when I was about 16 years old. Before that, I'd only played a little in gym class, never seriously. As it turned out, I was reasonably good at it right away. I wasn't tall or strong, but I had two things working in my favor. The first attribute was that years of moving hay bales on the farm had left my forearms so calloused that there was a near-zero chance of me feeling any pain or discomfort from a hard impact. The second? Springy legs. I could jump high enough to challenge players much taller than me.

Fast forward 25 years. I'd played on and off through my twenties and thirties, and after a few years off, I joined a charity tournament. Thankfully, the only person in the gym who knew me was my wife...because it did not go well. By day's end, my forearms stung. I kept hitting balls straight into the net. It seemed that nobody told my hitting arm that my legs could no longer boost me 36 inches in the air. After a slow dive-and-recovery off the wooden gym floor, my only fan screamed, 'You're forty, you fool!' She was right.

The ball and the net didn't care that I had bouncy legs, once upon a time. I should've adjusted my game. I was still playing like I was 18, while my body reminded me I wasn't. It took one rough day, and at least one injury, for me to learn a valuable lesson: anchoring.

In my case, my past abilities were irrelevant to my situation on the court. The pain, both physical and psychological, was a direct result of anchoring to outdated information.

In my "day job," I see the effects of anchoring all too often. Sometimes, an investor will anchor off of the original purchase price of an investment (as in, "I'll just get back to even."). More recently, an investor may fall victim to the temptation to anchor off of a "high water mark." Both of these data points are irrelevant to the present value of an investment and should not be considered in the decision of whether to buy, hold, or sell an asset.

COGNITIVE BIASES LEAD TO TRAGEDY

Few childhood memories are as seared into my mind as that January morning. I was in the third grade at my tiny rural elementary school. My entire class (of 50-60 students) gathered in one classroom with all three of the third-grade teachers. Someone wheeled in the big black cart with the one TV we had for the grade. It was around 11:30 in Upstate New York, the same time-zone as Cape Canaveral, Florida. As we did whenever we could, we all gathered around to watch a space shuttle launch out of Kennedy Space Center.

Every launch was cause for excitement back then. We'd scream our countdown, then yell 'Blastoff!' as the rocket launched. For many people, including the school staff, this event was particularly exciting because a teacher, Christa McAuliffe, was going into space.

Seventy-three seconds into its journey, the Space Shuttle Challenger came apart in mid-air, killing the entire seven-person crew. I still remember my social studies teacher sobbing as my classmates sat in stunned confusion. This wasn't how it was supposed to go. It was the first tragedy of its kind. The nation, stunned and grieving, demanded answers.

The primary cause was found to be the failure of specific parts named O-rings. Contributing factors included record-low temperatures on the morning of the launch. The President formed the Rogers Commission to investigate. They found that more than just equipment or weather were to blame. NASA's internal culture and its decision-making processes were also found to have contributed to the disaster. Test data had shown the potential for the O-rings to fail, but the issue was never seriously addressed. NASA Engineers' warnings about launching in cold temperatures were overlooked by management. A mix of human fallibility and toxic organizational culture contributed to a national tragedy.

These may be extreme examples of a few rather common cognitive biases that can affect any person or organization in their decision-making processes. These are Confirmation Bias and Groupthink. We should endeavor to identify these and whatever other biases may be shaping our decisions and develop systems for correcting them in real time. Let's start with the two that we've already named.

Confirmation Bias

We tend to notice the things that confirm what we already believe and ignore the rest. In the example of the Challenger, decision-makers may have focused on information that supported their desire to launch on time rather than that which pointed toward the risks of doing so.

An everyday example of confirmation bias may be a person who loves their pet dog and believes that she is the most wonderful animal to ever walk the earth (admittedly, I am this person). I am guilty of being far more likely to notice how sweetly she greets you at the door but conveniently ignore how she wakes up everyone in the house when she barks at a passing car in the night. I rush to defend her against any criticism.

Groupthink

When a team seems to desire a certain outcome, someone who disagrees with the consensus may hide their opinion in an effort to avoid conflict. This is how Groupthink can cause potentially better options to be overlooked. At NASA, investigators found that engineers with concerns about the o-rings were pressured to align with the organization's desire to stay on schedule. Their worries were essentially suppressed in the name of unity.

In a more mundane setting, we are all very likely to come across groupthink in the political landscape. The two major American political parties have become echo chambers where dissent is dismissed out of hand. This type of groupthink can lead to the reinforcement of extreme viewpoints or the prevention of alternative perspectives that might actually improve the party.

OTHER BIASES IN ACTION

In a 2011 article in the Harvard Business Review, professors Daniel Kahneman, Dan Lovallo, and Olivier Sibony addressed these and several other biases that can have harmful effects on strategic decision-making. Besides anchoring bias, confirmation bias, and groupthink, they also encouraged checking for things like self-interest, the affect heuristic, saliency bias, availability bias, and the halo effect.

Self-Interest Bias

Imagine the director of an organization who is interviewing candidates for a management position. She has two qualified candidates who could lead her team to new heights. If one candidate is clearly more talented and ambitious than the other, one would think that the hiring decision would be an easy one. Self-interest bias may lead to a bad decision; however, if the director takes into consideration that someday, a better candidate could be competing with her for her job! In the interest of preserving her position of authority, a self-interested hiring manager may choose the lesser job candidate. This would be to her benefit but likely the detriment of her organization, its employees, and its customers.

For a more concrete example of the damage done by self-interest bias, you need look no further than the Wells Fargo scandal that occurred around the year 2016. Managers and employees were encouraged to pursue their own interests in a way that came at the expense of the best interests of customers and eventually the reputation of the company. The pressure for employees to meet aggressive sales goals and earn rewards resulted in clients receiving unnecessary and/or unwanted accounts, credit cards, and loans. This culture was pushed beyond the bounds of common ethics when employees were found to have opened such accounts in clients' names without either their authorization or consent. Management clearly failed to provide adequate oversight, as is evidenced by years' worth of persistent unethical practices, despite numerous customer complaints. Allowing a culture of self-interest not only harmed customers but also caused Wells Fargo to face substantial legal and financial penalties.

The Affect Heuristic

Remember the last time that you ate at a chain restaurant. Think of something a bit better than fast food, but definitely not "fine dining." Do you remember what the menu looked like? It no doubt was filled with glossy pages featuring full-color photographs of several of the menu items. These businesses understand the potency of the affect heuristic. This bias leads us to rely on gut feelings or emotional reactions when making a decision. A colorful and appetizing photo may trigger a positive emotional response in the diner. The past experiences that one associates with the image may cause the dish to be far more appealing before you have even read the description, ingredients, or (gasp!) calorie count. In this situation, emotions might simply overrule the logic required for making the best decision.

In recent years, the affect heuristic may have contributed to the spread of COVID-19 in many regions. While mask-wearing was commonly recommended to help stop the spread of the illness, this notion was often met with a range of emotional responses. Whether an individual experienced anxiety or safety when wearing a mask, could easily shape the likelihood of their compliance with a mask mandate. Beyond masking, a person might allow emotional reactions to trump their belief in scientific evidence when deciding whether or not to get vaccinated. It is not difficult to see how the affect heuristic and its impact on people's behaviors may have increased the risk of COVID-19 transmission.

Saliency Bias

These days, it seems as if examples of saliency bias are everywhere! This cognitive bias is when people focus on the most easily noticeable information, potentially overlooking data points that are less conspicuous. The clearest example of this in the modern era may be "clickbait" headlines. With human attention being the most valuable commodity of the information age, eye-catching, sensationalistic, and shocking headlines are ever-present online. The increased likelihood that someone will engage with such intentionally attention-grabbing material is a common effect of saliency bias. While a user goes down internet rabbit holes of sensational content, they may be overlooking material of more practical importance like economics or local news. Being disproportionately exposed to emotionally charged content can result in a skewed perception of reality which can affect decision-making.

In my field of personal finance, saliency bias often rears its ugly head, resulting in the purchase of speculative investments by inexperienced investors. In the early 2020s, the media couldn't report enough about Non-Fungible Tokens (NFTs). Without getting into the complexities of the product itself, we can easily recognize how saliency bias contributed to the loss of a staggering amount of money. Over a million dollars was lost on one particular NFT that was purchased by celebrity

Justin Bieber. His "Bored Ape" NFT was valued at $1.3 million in 2022, and its price subsequently dropped to below $60,000 in mid-2023.

Bieber wasn't just burned by the NFT crash, but an example of how celebrity involvement may be a component of saliency bias that came up around digital products. The prevalence of sensational stories of people getting rich and the resulting FOMO (Fear of Missing Out) also contributed to the phenomenon. In the world of NFTs, several factors seemed to align to create a near-perfect case study in saliency bias. Unfortunately, ordinary citizens lost millions of dollars while learning firsthand why this particular bias is one to be wary of.

Availability Bias

Which is safer, walking to your destination or flying there? Many people are shocked to find that it is almost ten times safer to travel by air than it is to walk from place to place as a pedestrian. A person's lifetime odds of dying during air travel are 1 in 7,229, while only 1 in 749 as a pedestrian, according to a report from the National Safety Council (travel by automobile is substantially worse than either). If we consider the statistics per mile traveled, the difference is similarly dramatic. According to a 2013 National Highway Safety Administration report, there were only 0.07 fatalities per billion passenger miles flown. This means that a person could fly every day for a year and still only have a 1 in 85,000 risk of a fatality if they flew 500 miles each time. By the same metric (billions of miles traveled) in 2022, the Governors Highway Safety Association reported 2.37 deaths. This is to say that, by the mile, a person could be more than 33 times more likely to die as a pedestrian than an air passenger.

Seeing these statistics makes me wonder why the fear of flying is so prevalent. One explanation for this may be the availability bias. Availability bias happens when we rely too much on information that comes to mind easily. Plane crashes are big news. At the very least, they receive a great deal more media coverage than a story about a pedestrian death. The availability of frequent "evidence" of aviation accidents, as well as their dramatic nature, could lead to a disproportionate fear of flying versus statistically more dangerous modes of transportation like walking or driving. When choosing a mode of transportation, a traveler may choose an objectively more hazardous way to get to their destination simply because they can easily recall examples of plane crashes from their coverage in the media.

In the world of criminal justice, one could look at the existence of "Three-Strikes" laws as an example of how availability bias may lead to suboptimal decision-making. These laws mandate particularly harsh punishments for those convicted of three serious crimes. Laws like these are often a consequence of the public pressure resulting from the extensive media coverage of a crime with sensational details. This may be the case despite research suggesting that such laws do not reduce crime rates.

In 2011, Stanford Law School's "Three Strikes Project" found that almost 40% of inmates serving life sentences as a product of California's three strikes policy may not have deserved such harsh punishments. In less than two years following these findings, the project was able to overturn the life sentences of 26 people for reasons including mental illness, inadequate legal representation, and newly discovered evidence.

Simply put, vivid stories dominate our attention, even when the facts say otherwise. The wide reporting and repeated coverage of the details of a crime may make a single "date point" feel like a great deal more. Making a decision based on this perception is a textbook exercise in availability bias.

The Halo Effect

What do Supermodel Gisele Bündchen, comedian Larry David, and Baseball star David "Big Papi" Ortiz have in common? They are all examples of the dangers of the halo effect. More specifically, they all illustrate this phenomenon as it pertains to the failed FTX cryptocurrency exchange. In early 2023, while FTX CEO Sam Bankman-Fried faced criminal charges, celebrities like those listed above (as well as Tom Brady (NFL), Stephen Curry (NBA), Naomi Osaka (WTA), and Kevin O'Leary (Shark Tank)) were all facing lawsuits related to the collapse of FTX. Even though nobody could reasonably expect professional athletes and entertainers to be cryptocurrency experts, multiple complaints argued that they lent their credibility to FTX and thereby contributed to the loss of several billions of dollars to users of the exchange.

The halo effect is a cognitive bias that describes when our overall impression of someone shapes how we feel and think about their character. Our evaluation of one aspect of that person can transfer to our evaluation of the person as a whole.

In my lifetime, I've seen two American presidents whose resumes featured careers as a Hollywood actor and reality TV star. Examples of past interesting but unrelated jobs of members of Congress include an astronaut, a comedian, multiple actors, a musician, and a few pro athletes. The roster of past state Governors includes a professional bodybuilder (Schwarzenegger/California) and a professional wrestler (Ventura/Minnesota). The Halo Effect is clearly alive and well in the realm of politics!

Beyond the political sphere, in day-to-day life, the halo effect can influence our opinions in personal relationships. We may assume that an attractive person has other positive qualities, like intelligence or generosity. We often overlook red flags simply because we like what we see. At work, likeability can overshadow achievements when it comes to hiring decisions or performance evaluations. When making a purchase, who hasn't had an attractive salesperson attempt to increase the amount of money we spend? Examples are everywhere. Attractive people get the benefit of the doubt, even when they shouldn't.

CONCLUSION

This chapter explored how cognitive biases, often invisible, can quietly derail our decisions. Our examples included famous cases with tragic outcomes and more common situations where results may be more mundane. By recognizing and understanding these biases, we should be able to better mitigate their influence on our own decision-making in situations from those with the highest stakes to the more routine.

"Bias, like beauty, is often in the eye of the beholder. Facts are your firewall against bias."
—*Tom Brokaw*

TOOLS FOR YOUR KIT

KEY INSIGHT: Your brain is a meaning-making machine, but it's not always accurate. Knowing the most common cognitive biases helps you pause, reflect, and choose wisely.

MENTAL REFRAME: Your instincts are trying to help, but they don't always have the full picture. Treat gut feelings as a clue, not a conclusion.

PRACTICAL TOOL: Use the Bias Spotter Checklist to self-audit before major decisions. Watch out for:

- **Anchoring** – Fixating on the first piece of information
- **Confirmation Bias** – Favoring data that supports your beliefs
- **Groupthink** – Silencing dissent for harmony
- **Self-Interest Bias** – Letting your own gain skew your logic
- **Affect Heuristic** – Letting emotion override reason
- **Saliency Bias** – Overweighting flashy or dramatic info
- **Availability Bias** – Relying on recent or vivid examples
- **Halo Effect** – Letting one good trait color the whole picture

ACTION STEP: Next time you're making a choice, pause and ask: "Am I reacting... or deciding?" Then list one feeling you're having and one fact you know. Notice the difference.

BONUS TOOL: In moments of high emotion or low clarity, make it a habit to seek one outside data point, even if it contradicts your instinct. Let truth interrupt impulse.

CHAPTER 4

YOUR EDUCATION:

BE SMART ABOUT LEARNING

HIGHER EDUCATION doesn't just build knowledge; it shapes your future. Even as traditional learning evolves, I want to help guide you through the decisions that will shape your academic path. From challenging the conventional wisdom of "follow your passion" to taking a hard look at what schools really offer, this chapter provides a roadmap, urging you to question assumptions, embrace opportunities, and navigate the crossroads of academia. If you're deciding how, and whether, to pursue higher education, this chapter is for you.

EXAMINE YOUR ASSUMPTIONS
(YES, AGAIN)

Before we dive into education, let's borrow a key step from the chapter on choosing a partner. That is to examine any assumptions that you may have about furthering your education. Specifically, one should reflect on whether more education is truly what is needed to achieve one's desired future. If your goal is to start a luxury car detailing business, more formal schooling might not be the best use of your time or money. I don't recommend "burning the boats" on education, mind you. It's always a good idea to keep one's options open, but let's not be so foolish as to assume that a traditional degree from an accredited school is the answer for everyone. Certain futures may align better with vocational education, as in one who intends to work in the trades. Another possibility may be searching for an apprenticeship in your desired field. These days, online courses or certifications may also provide the most practical route to your eventual goal.

Having considered whether or not college is the answer, we might further contemplate the best timing for post-secondary education. After all, having kept the proverbial boats unburnt, we have preserved our ability to choose a more "traditional" degree program at a later date.

TIMING

Taking time off after high school, often called a "gap year," can offer major benefits. This could be a valuable time to gain insights and experiences that can enhance not only your personal development but also your future academic growth. A gap year can offer real benefits—time to explore, grow, and clarify what you really want. This, in turn, could lead to a more focused approach to future studies.

A gap year can also boost your credibility, especially if you gain real-world experience through work or service. Work or service experience can make you stand out from other college applicants and open up opportunities for acceptance into more prestigious institutions. Of course, I can't address the tangible benefits of work without talking about the money. A gap year can help you save for college and teach real financial skills through managing your own budget.

The benefits of time off between high school and college will vary from person to person. Time off isn't right for everyone, but it shouldn't be dismissed outright.

PASSION FIRST...OR MAYBE THIRD

"If you feel like there's something out there that you're supposed to be doing, if you have a passion for it, then stop wishing and just do it."
—Wanda Sykes

"OK. You can do that, but understand that no one owes you a living for it."
—Matt Miller

Wanda Sykes means well. As a successful comedian, it's easy to see why she tells people to follow their passion. It worked for her. But what about the rest of us, those who aren't wildly talented in a field that also happens to pay well?

Passion matters, but it shouldn't top your list of career questions. I propose the following two-question self-assessment to get you started on making this big decision.

Question #1:
What are you good at?

Billionaire entrepreneur Mark Cuban admits that his heart would have led him to a career as a professional athlete. Lacking the physical attributes and talent to make it in the big leagues, he instead built his career and his fortune in the field of technology. In the Amazon Insights for Entrepreneurs web series, Cuban said, "Everybody tells you, 'Follow your passion, follow your passion,'" but instead, he recommends focusing on what you're good at. He goes on to say, "When you look at where you put in your time, where you put in your effort, that tends to be the things that you are good at. And if you put in enough time, you tend to get really good at it."

NYU Professor, entrepreneur, and podcaster Scott Galloway also warns young people to lean away from following their passion. He recommends following one's talents and abilities, explaining that passion can be an effect rather than a cause. He proposes that "the recognition from colleagues, the money, the status will make you passionate about whatever it is." I'm sure the increased earnings from following your skills also wouldn't hurt.

Going back to Mark Cuban's youthful desire to make a living in professional athletics, one could argue that he eventually succeeded. In January of the year 2000, less than a year after he sold his internet radio company, Broadcast.com, Cuban purchased the majority stake in the NBA's Dallas Mavericks. Following his abilities allowed him to eventually pursue his passion in a big way.

Question #2:
Can it pay the bills and provide you
with the lifestyle you desire?

While we're challenging the romance of passion, let's rip off another Band-Aid: income matters. When I was at the age where I was choosing my educational path forward, I had a passion and some real skill for playing footbag (sometimes called "hacky sack"). Unfortunately, very few people in the world make a living by kicking a small object in the air over and over again. But no matter how much I loved it, footbag wasn't going to pay the bills. Thank goodness I have always been good with numbers and could explain complex topics to people in an understandable way. These existing traits, along with the knowledge I gained in a formal educational setting, prepared me to begin my career in personal finance.

EVALUATING YOUR EDUCATIONAL PATHS

Now, assume that you have determined if college is the right path for you and you've decided on your timing. You can process the evaluation of abilities, passions, life goals, and earning potential to narrow down your list of potential courses of study. Talk to people who can answer your questions and raise the ones you haven't thought to ask. Here is a short list of such people:

- **Undergraduate Students** - get a feel for what life in the major is actually like.
- **Grad Students** - gain insight from someone deeply committed to that field.
- **Working Professionals** - see what the job looks like long-term.
- **Professors** - learn what the field demands and how it connects to real life.

CHOOSING A SCHOOL

Choosing a school is a big decision. You're committing years of your life and, often, a lot of money. Once you know your field, make sure the school's programs align with it. In the name of not "burning the boats," you might also wish to see if your second and third choices would be available to you there.

For most majors, it is a good idea to verify that the university is accredited. This may be key in ensuring that potential employers and other educational institutions recognize the work you've done there. After meeting this basic requirement, you can consider some more specific details.

Having covered the basic criteria, it is time to consider more specifically where to study. Let's look at this question in a very literal sense first. The physical location of a school could come with a great deal of both benefits and drawbacks. Proximity to a support network of friends and family may be important to some students. Are you more suited for life in an urban, suburban, or rural setting? Is there a benefit to studying internationally? Lastly, the cost of living in the area could dramatically affect your quality of life over your college career.

Look beyond just tuition. What's the total cost, including housing, transportation, fees, books, and everyday living? To what extent can these costs be offset by grants, scholarships, financial aid, or income from work-study or part-time employment?

What does all of that tuition money pay for anyway? Is the college hiring top-tier faculty? Are the labs filled with the latest in advanced technology and equipment? I suggest you tour the campus with an exacting eye. Given how expensive college is today, it's only fair to expect the highest standards in most, if not all of, the following:

- **Academic Buildings** - These should have modern classrooms with the latest audiovisual technology. There should be specialized laboratories for sciences and studios for the arts.
- **Library** - The library facilities should have extensive collections of both physical and digital materials. They should provide access to a robust list of periodicals, journals, and databases. Libraries should provide both quiet study spaces and areas better suited for collaborative work.
- **Housing** - On-campus accommodations should be comfortable and well-maintained. Public spaces should be well-lit at night.
- **Health and Wellness Centers** - Facilities should include not only health clinics for medical services but also counseling and mental health support.
- **Transportation** - Look for bike racks and walking paths. Many campuses will also have shuttle services and/or easy access to public transportation.
- **Safety and Security** - Are there emergency phone boxes that are easy to spot around campus? Campus police and security workers should seem ever-present.

This list is not meant to be comprehensive but a good starting point as you assemble your checklist of desirable features for a college campus. I realize that I didn't mention collegiate sports or the wild parties. I assume that any student looking for those won't need my help to find them.

LIFE AFTER ACADEMIA

The main reason for higher education? A fulfilling career. Taking a look at graduate employment rates is a sensible first step in figuring out whether a specific school is likely to be an ideal launching pad for your professional future. Research the percentage of graduates who secure employment in their field shortly after graduation. High employment rates can indicate a university's success in preparing students for the job market. Also look at the success of past students. Have alumni gone on to do what you want to do? Those who have succeeded in their careers can be a positive sign of the institution's impact.

Who You Know

During a student's period of study, they may be provided with networking opportunities like alumni networks, career fairs, and dedicated networking events. These might all help establish useful connections with professionals in a chosen field.

Also, before graduation, students may be able to get a career "head start" by gaining work experience through internships, co-ops, and work-study programs. Real-world experience can greatly enhance your employability, so check if the school has strong connections with industries and offers programs like the ones mentioned above. Also, prospective students should evaluate what job placement services may be available to them.

Further Formal Education

Some students won't go straight into work; they're planning for grad school. If you plan to pursue further education after your degree, check the availability and quality of graduate programs at the university that you have in mind. Beyond the items mentioned above, it makes sense to consider the following additional items:

- **Research Opportunities** - Working on research projects can strengthen your graduate school application, so you should consider the availability of such opportunities.
- **Graduate School Placement Rates** - This would be your equivalent measure to the job placement rates mentioned in earlier paragraphs. Find out the percentage of undergraduates from the university who go on to reputable graduate programs. A high rate may be an indication that a school has a good method for preparing students for advanced studies.

- **Support Services for Grad School Preparation** - Does the institution offer specific services to help students prepare for graduate school applications? Such services may include workshops or the availability of one-on-one advisor relationships.

OFF AND RUNNING

Once you're in school, remember: you can still adjust. Few decisions are permanent. You have a long road ahead of you, and your path may change, no matter how much time and energy you have put into your prior decisions. For this reason, I recommend that you start your education with more general courses and slowly become more specific in your studies over time. This will preserve some flexibility as you continue to learn more and more about your chosen field and the alternatives. Speaking of alternatives, I recommend you begin and maintain open ongoing dialogues with those who are engaged in other areas of study. Perhaps the resulting conversations will help you discover a future that you previously did not know existed. Never stop evaluating and making adjustments as you move through this journey. Start broad, then specialize. Talk to students outside your major. Stay curious.

CONCLUSION

Remember, you are not just at the end of a chapter but at the threshold of better educational choices. In the considerations explored, from the timing of educational pursuits to scrutinizing institutions and evaluating post-graduate prospects, the call to action resonates. Varied voices, from industry titans like Mark Cuban to comedienne Wanda Sykes, call you to not merely follow a predetermined path but to forge your own. As you stand at the intersection of passion, aptitude, and pragmatism, consider this an invitation to embrace the malleability of your journey. Your future is a collection of unwritten chapters that are yours alone to write, a story of continual evaluation, adaptation, and the pursuit of knowledge.

TOOLS FOR YOUR KIT

KEY INSIGHT: College is one of the most expensive and most defaulted decisions people make. The right path starts by asking if you need it before asking where to go.

MENTAL REFRAME: College isn't a rite of passage. It's an investment. Like any big investment, it deserves critical thinking, not auto-pilot.

PRACTICAL TOOL: Use the 3-Phase Inquiry Method to make a deliberate education decision:

1. Start with Big Questions
   o Do I really need college for the life I want?
   o Is now the right time or would I benefit from working, traveling, or interning first?
2. Choose Your Path Wisely
   o What am I good at?
   o Can this path pay the bills sustainably?
   o What does success look like for me?
3. Investigate Options Deeply
   o Visit campuses.
   o Ask real students and graduates about their experience.
   o Compare not just tuition, but total cost and debt load versus post-grad outcomes.

ACTION STEP: Make a one-page College Decision Brief. Include:

- Your top 3 reasons for attending
- 2 viable alternatives to college
- What would success look like five years after graduation

BONUS TOOL: Before committing, talk to three people further down the path you're considering (students, professors, or working professionals). Ask them, "Would you do it again?"

CHAPTER 5

ADAPTING TO CHANGING CONDITIONS:
THE SIMPLICITY IN COMPLEXITY

THE IMAGE OF SOME YOKEL chewing straw is cliché, but sometimes clichés are earned. In my youth, I lived that cliché, proof that some stereotypes exist for a reason. My rule was simple: If Jimmy chewed hay, I chewed hay. Jimmy ran the hay farm where I worked summers from the age of 12 to about 21. Truth be told, I never knew then why either of us was chewing hay. I didn't know if we were checking for texture or taste. Turns out, it was both. It depended on the time of day.

There was always plenty of work to do around the farm, but a few weeks of each summer were dedicated to the hay crop. This involved mowing hay, tedding it (spreading it out to dry), raking it into rows, baling it, and stacking those bales into storage areas. The steps were always the same, but the timing was critical. Sometimes, a good chew could help decide when to do what.

In the morning, around sunrise, when the sugar content of the plants is the highest, is when you want to cut it. Later in the day, after the hay has had time to dry, you can pull some hay from the bottom of a wind-row. The amount that it crunches and snaps when you chew it can indicate whether it is ready to bale. Ideally, the day is sunny, and a gentle breeze would be a plus.

Like the old saying goes, 'Make hay while the sun shines' because once the rain comes, it's too late. Rain on cut hay ruins it. Rain washes out nutrients, breaks down the leafy parts, and eventually causes the hay to rot. Prolonged rain on hay that is lying in the field can make the eventual bales go from being high-quality feed for thoroughbred horses to being good for little more than archery targets.

Once the hay is cut and lying in the field, you can use the tedder to spread it out, but only if you're confident that it won't get rained on. If there is a threat of light rain in the morning, it may be better to run the tedder afterward. This way, you can not only spread it out to dry in the sun but also use the process to shake off the moisture that may be on the top layer of the crop. Other things may occur between the manual steps of the hay baling process and are similarly out of your control, but you must have a plan for each of them. If you're in the business of hay farming, your responses to changing conditions can make a great deal of difference, not only in the quality of your product but how many bales you will eventually be able to sell.

You may be saying, "This is interesting and all, but why does it matter to me?"

Hay farming is a multi-step process shaped by forces you can't control. This type of process is not uncommon in life, so it would be best if we had a tool to give ourselves the highest probability of a desirable outcome. That same cycle, of acting, observing, and adapting, also shows up in strategy games.

Even Chess isn't Chess

"This is chess, it ain't checkers."
—Alonzo to Jake, "Training Day"

Denzel Washington delivered the line above on his way to winning a Best Actor Academy Award for his portrayal of Alonzo Harris in Training Day. The purpose of this line was to convey the notion that their work was not simple but rather involved complex strategy and tactics. They had to not only see the bigger picture but also anticipate their opponents' future moves. Both chess and checkers are played on a board made of 64 squares of alternating colors. Checkers all move the same. In chess, every piece has its own powers and its own rules. When considering the potential combinations of moves available in a chess match, it has been stated (and confirmed) that there are more potential move variations in a game of chess than there are atoms in the observable universe!

Every move in chess is a decision that needs to be made. With so many possibilities, how does anyone even decide their first move? How have some players reached the level of Grandmaster, much less the 40 or so who have achieved Super Grandmaster status? Understanding how great players choose moves can teach us about decision-making in life.

TWO WAYS OF THINKING

Many believe chess masters think 30 moves ahead. While it may be possible in some simple cases, it is rarely done. Five-time World Chess Champion Magnus Carlsen, who says that he can see about 15 moves ahead (and occasionally 20), is considered by many to be the strongest player in the history of the game. In reality, great players rely more on pattern recognition and instinct than raw calculation. Over countless hours of study and practice, they have developed an intuitive understanding of the spatial relationships on the board.

In his book "Thinking Fast and Slow," Nobel Prize-winning economist Daniel Kahneman described how people think and avoid poor decisions. He introduced two distinct "systems" that we all use. The first is slow and deliberate, and the other is quicker and based more on intuition and a less specific sense of a situation. When called upon, a chess grandmaster can choose between and use the more appropriate method of thinking through a position, or perhaps a combination of both.

DECISION TREES

In his book "How Life Imitates Chess," former World Chess Champion (1985-2000) Garry Kasparov introduces his reader to a tool called the "Decision Tree." This is a way of identifying the many potential paths forward that result from a decision or chess move. Once identified, a decision tree can help a person decide which move to make next. The first player to move a piece in a chess game has 20 possible moves that are legal to make. Their opponent then has 20 possible replies. You may see how the math works to get from these initial numbers to the mind-boggling number that surpasses the number of atoms in the known universe! On average, each player can make about 40 possible moves from a chess position. That means that after each player has taken their turn, there are potentially 1600 (40x40) positions that can result. After two moves, there are roughly 2.5 million possible positions. That number surpasses 4 billion after 3 moves! How in the world can someone decide what to do next with so many possibilities?!

Think of a tree, where each branch is a possible path forward. Some lead to fruit; others to dead ends. Each possible choice would be represented by a new branch coming from the trunk. The possibilities from that new position would then be represented by smaller branches that split off from the initial branch. This visualization exercise can continue with branch upon branch until that singular trunk has more tiny twigs in the air than we could reasonably count. Our job now is quite simple. We need to start sawing off branches.

Not all options are equal. Some lead to disaster. So prune those branches early. In chess, there are decisions a player can make that will immediately lose them a valuable piece or grant their opponent an insurmountable advantage. These choices can immediately be discarded, and those branches pruned from the decision tree. In life, we can simply rule out the obviously foolish options when facing complex choices. In both life and chess, we can use our more intuitive brain functions to narrow our options down to what we can determine to be the best three or four choices. Once you have this short list established, it is time to start working down the tree branches. By asking what will happen next…and next…and next, a person can look for potential pitfalls and use those insights to eliminate the worst option of those that remain. Once you know a path is a dead end, stop walking it. One should repeat this process until one of two outcomes emerges. Either all of the flawed options are eliminated until the best one remains, or one tree branch reveals such an irresistible reward as to make it the clear path forward. From this point, the next step can be taken confidently.

THE SIMPLE BECOMES SIMPLER

Maybe chess isn't your game. With 32 pieces and 64 squares, it can feel overwhelming. So let's simplify things and look at a smaller decision tree, built around a game nearly everyone knows. What's simpler than Tic-Tac-Toe? (Or "Noughts and Crosses," if you're in England.) Two identical pieces. One simple goal: get three in a row on a 3x3 board.

Here's the bad news: there are over 250,000 possible games of Tic-Tac-Toe. Not so simple after all. But here's the good news: that massive number comes from treating every move as unique, even when many are basically the same. It is true that there are 9 possible first moves in a game, 8 ways for an opponent to reply, and so on. Actually, you only have three real choices for your first move: the center, a corner, or a side square. There's only one center square, but all four corners are strategically the same. They are identical, in fact, if we are willing to simply tilt our heads or rotate the game board. Just like that, the top left corner can be any other corner on the board!

The second move sounds more complicated, but maybe it isn't. If you are the second player to move and the first move is to the center, you only have a choice between two replies, not eight. You can choose a corner or a side; either way, symmetry makes many of those options effectively the same.

More replies are available if the first move was not to claim the center, but the basic concept still applies. The idea is that this decision is not as complicated as it may seem at first glance. If the first move is a corner, it looks like there are eight replies, but functionally, it's really just five. The options for the second player are center square, corner across from the original corner, corner adjacent to the original corner, side square adjacent, or side square not adjacent. Again, if we stop worrying about choices that are practically the same, we can prune our decision tree, leaving a clearer path and more confidence in the next step.

Now consider this: a full game of Tic-Tac-Toe has a maximum of nine moves, or four decisions per player (placing your mark in the last available open square doesn't count as a decision). Eventually, each decision becomes easier than the last. This is because of a combination of two factors. The first is that there are few available spaces to choose from. The second is that the outcomes of some options will lead to an immediate victory or a loss. Your job? Make the obvious good move and avoid the bad ones. If you already have two in row, make it three. If the opponent has two in a row, block them.

THE BEST WAY

Here's the good news and bad news about Tic-Tac-Toe. The good? It's a solved game. That means the outcome can be predicted with certainty if both players make flawless moves. The bad news? You can play perfectly and still not win. If both players follow the optimal strategy, the game ends in a draw. The upside? If you play it right, you'll never lose.

In a 1993 issue of Cognitive Science, psychologists Kevin Crowley and Robert S. Siegler published a study titled "Flexible Strategy Use in Young Children's Tic-Tac-Toe." Their work built on an early AI program from 1972, created by scientists Allen Newell and Herbert A.

Simon. That AI followed eight simple rules, each triggered by the available spaces on the board. A human could win, or at least avoid losing, by following those same rigid rules.

For example: If you're the second player, take the center square if it's open. If the center's already taken, grab a corner. This example proves a key point in decision-making science: If someone's already solved the problem, follow their lead. Don't waste time reinventing a proven solution.

Chess, unlike Tic-Tac-Toe, is not a solved game and likely won't be for a long time. Yet even now, the best chess engines can defeat the world's top Super Grandmasters. That doesn't make chess knowledge useless. Far from it. We now have a treasure trove of strategy, gleaned from computers and grandmasters alike.

"THERE'S A FUNNY LINE"
— ERIC ROSEN, INTERNATIONAL MASTER

Professional Chess Player and International Master, Eric Rosen, is known by his fans for his exceptional chess opening preparation. When Rosen knows who he's playing, he studies their past games to uncover patterns, then prepares openings designed to exploit them. A "line" in chess is a specific, proven sequence of moves that aims to achieve a favorable position. Over decades of competition, Rosen has memorized countless lines. Thanks to his encyclopedic recall, Rosen can play entire sequences, move after move, straight from memory, even against a surprise opponent. In his YouTube video "My Deepest Opening Preparation in the Queen's Gambit Declined," Rosen plays 20 moves against a strong opponent, then casually says, "This is still prep." During the game, he references a match by fellow International Master Kassa Korley, playing the same line, move for move. Later, he even recalls one of his own past games, naming the opponent and event with striking accuracy.

This kind of recall might seem superhuman, but it's not unique to Rosen. Many elite chess players, especially those who stream, show similar, almost eerie recall of game history. Rosen's fans know to expect fireworks when he says, "There's a funny line," while playing.

Luckily, you don't need Rosen's memory to benefit from the lines left behind by others. When life demands a decision, look to those who've faced it before and won. Ask friends. Talk to mentors. Read. Search. The map is out there, you just have to look. With luck, you'll find a master decision-maker, someone whose "line" shows you the best way forward.

CONCLUSION

Whether in chess or life, choices can feel endless. Like a grandmaster staring down a cluttered chessboard, we face complex decisions that demand careful thought. Fortunately, guiding principles can bring clarity in the fog of uncertainty.

Chess strategy offers more than game insight; it reveals how we approach decisions in life. From deep calculation to gut instinct, we saw how good decisions blend logic with intuition. Decision trees offer a roadmap: prune the bad branches, and what's left is your best path forward.

Even Tic-Tac-Toe teaches strategy. With every move, pattern recognition and planning come into play. With every move, the tree branches and the right choices become clearer. Just like in life, games offer lessons, experience, and insight, and proven strategies can guide us to better outcomes.

In life, as in chess, there are lines, paths forged by those who've navigated similar decisions before. From chess openings to mentor advice, we can lean on the wisdom of those who've walked the road before us. Even when choices feel chaotic, there are tools and strategies to guide you.

TOOLS FOR YOUR KIT

🔑 **KEY INSIGHT:** Not all decisions deserve the same level of effort. Some need instinct. Others demand rigor. The smartest thinkers know when to go fast, when to go slow and, how to blend both.

🌀 **MENTAL REFRAME:** SPEED isn't sloppy, and slowness isn't smart. Trust quick decisions when the cost of failure is low. Go slow when the price of a mistake is high.

🔧 **PRACTICAL TOOL:** Use the Fast vs. Slow Thinking Filter:

- Fast Thinking: Great for familiar, low-risk, or time-sensitive situations (e.g., buying groceries, setting a meeting time).
- Slow Thinking: Essential for complex, costly, or emotionally loaded choices (e.g., quitting a job, getting married).
- Blended Thinking: Start fast, then double-check with slow logic, or vice versa.

Then apply the Decision Tree Framework:

- List all options
- Eliminate obvious bad ones
- Group duplicates or overlapping paths
- For each remaining branch, project the next step
- Choose the branch with the most promising or least harmful outcome

✅ **ACTION STEP:** Take a current decision and build a quick decision tree:

- 3–5 branches
- 1–2 levels deep
- Circle the branch you'd feel most relieved to take today

🔨 **BONUS TOOL:** Don't reinvent the wheel. Ask:

- Has someone solved this already?
- Is there a blueprint I can follow?
- Who has walked this path, and what did they learn?

CHAPTER 6

GEOGRAPHIC STRATEGY:
WHERE YOU ARE SHAPES
WHO YOU BECOME

ASK SOMEONE TO NAME their biggest decisions, and they'll probably list marriage, school, or career. But one of the most overlooked is where to live. If Chapter 4 was about what to do and Chapter 2 about who to do it with, then this chapter asks: Where should you go to do it all?

First, let us revisit a useful practice from Chapters 2 and 4. This is where we question our preexisting assumptions. Many people assume they'll live their whole lives near where they were born, but that belief can limit opportunities. In August of 2023, All Star Home surveyed 1,000 people. Their results revealed:

- 29% still live in their hometown.
- Over 40% of that group plan to stay there for life.
- Among those who moved, the average distance was just 30 miles.

Of the people who did move out of town, 70% said they felt they needed to leave to "live the life they wanted." Among the reasons that some people stayed put were comfort, emotional attachment, and a fear of the unknown.

That same year, a LendingTree survey of nearly 2,000 Millennials and Gen Z respondents (ages 18–42) found that 57% of them lived in their hometowns. The number goes up to 62% if you include those who are outside of the town itself but still close to their parents. When asked why respondents chose to stay so close to where they were raised, the most popular answer was "Family obligation, not preference, was the top reason, cited by 42%. Only 29% chose the reply, indicating that they stayed because they "Don't want to leave."

> *"If you feel stuck, move. You're not a tree."*
> *—Germany Kent*

If you let go of attachments to where you were raised and start fresh, how do you narrow down a world of possibilities? Let's return to the PRism Protocol as our lens.

Principles

If we start from a place of your core values, we may find that the world of options quickly turns into a short list of potential homes. For many people, their ethics and morals stem from their faith. If this is true for you, then having a community that shares your spiritual beliefs may be very important to you. If community and shared beliefs matter, that may point clearly to certain places. For example, members of the LDS Church may be more likely to live in Utah. Specifically, the area around Salt Lake City has a high concentration of LDS members, and the resulting culture affects various aspects of life, including social activities, community organizations, and local policies. People looking for Amish Communities may first consider specific areas in Pennsylvania, Ohio, and Indiana. A little research can reveal ideal communities for any number of different faith groups from the "Bible Belt" in the American South to some of the majority Jewish neighborhoods in Brooklyn.

Beyond spirituality, one might look for locations that align with their values as they pertain to certain social issues, personal convictions reflected in regional legislation, or diversity. One's own definition of principles may include different deeply held philosophies, morals, ethics, or simple integrity in decision-making. As we consider making the geographic decision from the inside out, these core ideas should not be taken lightly.

Priorities

At different times in my life, I traveled almost every day for my work. This made proximity to a major airport a priority for our family. It not only determined what city or town I would live in, but also what neighborhoods made the most sense. Access to walking trails mattered since we enjoy taking our dogs out for a bit of exercise. For families with children, proximity to a playground or quality schools may top the list.

Easy access to quality healthcare facilities could affect the decisions of someone undergoing treatment for an ongoing condition.

Preferences

I no longer fly weekly for work, but I still travel for fun a few times a year. I would prefer to live closer to an international airport than I do today, but other priorities make it so we do not. I prefer being close to snowcapped mountains, and my wife likes to be near saltwater. We can live in a place where both of these occur naturally (and quite beautifully), and those preferences overruled the former. Sadly, despite my strong preference to the contrary, I don't even live in a state that houses a professional basketball team!

> *"Those who know me know I'm passionate about lists, and top of my list of priorities is my family. My wife Joan and I do not consider our legacy to our children to be wealth or fame but the opportunity to pursue happiness by following their own path."*
> *— Sir Richard Branson*

To apply the PRism Protocol, start by making a list. Write each of your Principles, Priorities, and Preferences on a sticky note or index card. This lets you move and reorder them easily.

As you build out your list, the latter approach will make it easier for you to slide items up or down your list. You may even find the things you thought were priorities slide down into the category of simple preferences. Of course, families will want to consider the input of different family members, and a discussion or perhaps a series of negotiations will help to determine the eventual list. Similarly, you will want to work and rework the appropriate "rankings" of the various items. The end result should provide a clearer set of guidelines for how you can make this important decision in a way that best serves your future.

> *"I don't want to be a product of my environment.*
> *I want my environment to be a product of me."*
> *— Frank Costello, as played by Jack Nicholson in The Departed*

So far, we have framed the choice surrounding your geographic location as an effort to choose a place that is best suited to you. This would be a good time to once again examine the assumptions that we had already made before even beginning the process. This is that you are looking for a location that is already ideal in some ways. Instead of chasing the "perfect" place... what if you built one?

Over the last several years, I have more frequently been in conversations with people who intentionally move to places that do not quite match their principles or priorities but could someday. I've met passionate liberals and conservatives who purposely moved to "purple" states, places where their votes and voices carry more weight. In this way, as a swing voter in a swing state, they might have a larger impact on the world around them.

In the area of social issues, I have similarly seen people intentionally opt for the struggle of working against a local status quo to help shape their surroundings and affect their friends and neighbors. This type of life is not easy and certainly not for everyone, but it can be quite rewarding for someone who prioritizes making a difference in their community and the world.

This type of transformational thinking might eventually yield tangible financial rewards as well. By getting ahead of the curve on migration, growth, or development you may be investing not just in a place, but in your future. This could benefit you in the long run through career advancement or business profitability for an entrepreneur. Home purchasers may see property values rise meaningfully.

For those with some foresight and a certain risk tolerance, several benefits may come from moving to a place where trends show it is becoming more ideal, rather than one that current data show is already so. When asked about his remarkably successful hockey career, arguably the greatest player of all time, Wayne Gretzky famously replied, "I skate to where the puck is going to be, not where it has been."

DOLLARS AND CENTS

Let's now take a closer look at the financial side of where you live. Where you live can profoundly shape your financial future.

Job Prospects

A survey of 4000 people by the worldwide employment website, Indeed, revealed that 45% of people who relocated during the 1-year study period did so for occupational reasons. Of those, the majority indicated that a stronger job market was a key motivation. Many stated their reasons as being better opportunities to build their skills or simply increased compensation.

Much like in our earlier discussion around faith communities, certain occupational specialties also lend themselves to specific locations. The job prospects for a sea captain can be rather limited for a person living in Kansas, after all. One industry famous for its specific clusters of opportunities is technology. A computer programmer wishing to fast-track their immediate earnings and long-term career potential might choose to move to Silicon Valley in California or the Seattle area. Just as an actor may move to Los Angeles or a country singer to Nashville, a person who works in public policy may gravitate towards settling down near Washington, DC. A person who is fluent in Spanish may find a longer list of job opportunities in an area like Miami, which houses the Latin American operations for several large corporations.

Taxes

There may be more reasons than making use of your Spanish language skills to move to a state like Florida. Florida is one of nine states in the United States that do not levy a state income tax against its citizens. Moving to one of these states from a state that does take a piece of your income for tax purposes can feel like receiving an immediate pay raise!

As I write this, the nine states without a state income tax are:

- Alaska
- Florida
- Nevada
- New Hampshire
- South Dakota
- Tennessee
- Texas
- Washington
- Wyoming

Depending on a person's station in life, however, other components of the tax code may mean more to them than the income tax rate. Someone may be in a stage in life where they are doing a great deal of accumulation. This may mean furnishing their new home, purchasing vehicles, or buying expensive tools and equipment. If their spending is relatively high compared to their taxable income, they may seek out a place with minimal sales tax. Currently, there are five states with no general statewide sales tax. These are:

- Alaska
- Delaware
- Montana
- New Hampshire
- Oregon

Much later in life, there may be a tax consideration that won't necessarily affect you but could certainly affect future generations of your family. For those beyond a certain level of wealth at the time of their passing, their heirs may be faced with having to pay an inheritance tax to the state, or the estate itself could have to pay an estate tax. Several states have no estate tax or inheritance tax at the time of this writing. One of those taxes may be an issue if you live in one of 17 states or the District of Columbia. The two states with the highest current levels of estate taxation are Washington and Hawaii, with rates that go as high as 20%.

Cost of Living

Having discussed how geography can affect how much money you earn, we moved on to how much you get to keep after taxes. It only stands to reason that we should now examine what determines how much you are left with after all of your bills and day-to-day expenses have been paid. Things like the costs of healthcare, housing, utilities, and transportation all contribute to the larger category of expenses labeled the "cost of living." Higher pay doesn't always mean more money, especially if costs are higher, too.

Unfortunately, so many factors go into calculating the cost of living for an area that there is no universally accepted measurement by which we can compare potential home areas. Some organizations and individuals have come up with some creative ways to help a person gauge the affordability of an area, though. In 1986, The Economist Magazine introduced a lighthearted tool called "The Big Mac Index." The concept was that the cost of a standardized product that was available almost everywhere could be a fair way to assess how relatively affordable an area was. Of course, this tool was limited in its utility, but it did a fair job of introducing the diverse readership of The Economist to the concept of relative cost of living. Over time, various other publications and organizations have devised their own indices to compare the relative cost of living between different places. They typically consider factors like groceries, housing, transportation, and other goods and services. These include the following:

- **Mercer (consulting firm)** - Their index considers the cost of over 200 individual items in cities around the world.
- **Economist Intelligence Unit (EIU)** - This division of The Economist Group publishes its own Worldwide Cost of Living Index.

- **U.S. Bureau of Economic Analysis (BEA)** - This group built tools for better understanding the cost-of-living differences within the United States. They are called Regional Price Parities (RPPs)
- **Chambers of Commerce and Economic Development Offices** - Before choosing to move to an area, it may be worthwhile to reach out to some local organizations that may have cost of living reports specific to that region.
- **Numbeo** - The last resource on that list is a bit non-traditional insofar as it is a crowdsourced database. Their cost of living index aggregates user-contributed data to compare the affordability of different areas.

CONCLUSION

Choosing the right place to live is a deeply personal decision shaped by a combination of principles, priorities, and preferences. By using the PRism Protocol to clarify what truly matters to you, you can narrow down your options and make an informed choice that aligns with your values and lifestyle. Whether you seek a community that reflects your beliefs, prioritize practical considerations like job opportunities and cost of living, or dream of a location that fulfills your personal preferences, this decision represents an opportunity to shape your future. While geographic decisions are complex, by approaching them thoughtfully and with intention, you can create an environment that not only supports your current needs but also nurtures the best version of your future.

TOOLS FOR YOUR KIT

🔑 **KEY INSIGHT:** Where you live shapes how you think, feel, work, and connect. Geography is not just background; it's a variable you can adjust to create better odds.

🌀 **MENTAL REFRAME:** You're not a tree. You're allowed to move. Staying where you are may feel familiar, but it isn't always what's best.

🔧 **PRACTICAL TOOL:** Revisit the PRism Protocol with geography in mind:

- **Principles:** Does your current environment align with your core values?
- **Priorities**: Does it support your goals in terms of career, family, health, lifestyle?
- **Preferences:** Are you clinging to comforts that no longer serve you?

Explore Place Economics before making a move:

- Job prospects
- State and local income taxes
- Sales tax
- Inheritance/estate taxes
- Cost of living (housing, groceries, transportation)

☑️ **ACTION STEP:** Pick three locations you're curious about. For each one, write down:

- A lifestyle perk
- A financial consideration
- A possible downside

Then ask: Which tradeoffs are you most willing to live with?

🎁 **BONUS TOOL:** Make a list of the things you'd gain emotionally and practically by staying where you are. Then list what you might gain by leaving. Sometimes clarity comes not from logic, but from seeing it all laid out.

CHAPTER 7

RISK SYMMETRY:
WHEN THE ODDS LIE

EARLY IN THIS BOOK, I shared a story about pulling my wife across the street, resulting in just a worse "seat" to a surprise flash mob. There may not have been a clear 'right' choice, but I don't regret choosing caution. On the surface, the cost of moving was just a slightly worse view of the show, and the upside to staying was potentially the proverbial "best seat in the house." In hindsight, moving may seem like a poor choice, but that view ignores the role of risk.

We now know that it was absolutely safe to stay in the middle of the action, but at the moment, I was not so sure. My worst-case scenario? A violent attack. If inaction could have led to trauma, injury, or worse, then giving up a good view was a small price for peace of mind.

I don't know if anyone has the statistics surrounding the probability of witnessing a flash mob (do people still do those?) versus witnessing a public act of violence, but the math geek in me is curious about how those two likelihoods would compare. The loving husband in me doesn't care about the math. There is simply no potential upside that can outweigh the potential of harm to someone I love. As useful as data is, real-life decisions often come with murkier waters and higher stakes.

DEAL OR NO DEAL

The American game show Deal or No Deal shouldn't have worked on paper. Yet it ran for 234 episodes between 2005 and 2019. The show was based on a Dutch concept that was introduced in the year 2000 and inspired international versions in over 80 countries. The American version stopped recording new episodes several years ago, and yet even today, reruns air around the clock. Another spin-off, "Deal or No Deal Island," is scheduled to premiere in 2024. It's a simple concept, but it's captivated millions worldwide for decades.

In the United States version, 26 briefcases are displayed on a stage. Each case has a number inside, signifying its cash value, and these range from one penny to one million dollars. No one can tell the amounts in the cases, and they are randomly assigned. The contestant chooses one case to place beside them, and throughout the game, they then choose cases to have opened and discarded from the game. This eliminates their chance to win the specific sum displayed inside the discarded cases. Ideally, for the contestant, they would choose the highest number to be deemed "their case" first, and proceed to eliminate the smallest numbers until they are found to be left holding the top prize.

While this concept alone might get a few viewers, it would probably not be terribly popular, and the episodes would be extremely short. What makes "Deal or No Deal" such a hit is the drama that occurs when they are periodically presented with an offer to take a cash amount and quit the game. The offer is always some percentage of the average of the amounts that are still eligible to be won by the contestant. The decision then becomes a battle between an individual's fear of losing the guaranteed amount offered to them and a combination of greed and optimism about their chances of winning an amount higher than the offer. They announce, "Deal" to accept the cash offer and end the game or "No Deal" to keep playing and eliminate more cases.

The goal of this book is to help people to make better decisions, and what is an episode of "Deal or No Deal" if not a repeated public case study on how people make decisions? Thankfully, years of gameplay provide abundant data to determine if good decisions were made. Every offer came down to a simple question: Was it a good deal? This shouldn't be difficult since determining the expected value of what is in a case is a function of pretty simple math. If we take the simplest example, we can imagine that there are only two cases left in play, and the amounts inside are $10 and $200,000. The contestant has exactly a 50/50 shot of going home with either amount. A mathematically fair offer for a case in this scenario would be $100,005, determined by adding the total amounts and dividing by the number of cases in play ($200,010/2). Any amount below that amount is not a fair offer and should theoretically be refused, while any higher offer should be accepted.

Now that we know how to calculate whether an offer is good or bad mathematically, it would make sense to review how fair the offers have been on the episodes that have aired. Spoiler alert: most of the offers were mathematically bad deals. More specifically, over 80% of the televised offers were for less than the calculated fair expected value of an unopened case at that specific point in the game. Moreover, a fair or good deal has never been offered to a contestant who had more than 6 cases remaining. I suspect the economics of producing a game show offers an incentive to keep someone playing the game longer.

Knowing the odds, there's one obvious rule: don't take a deal with more than six cases left. Historically and mathematically, these have not been good deals for the player. After all, your odds of winning an amount lower than the offer are greater than your odds of winning an amount greater than the offer. This situation is one of "asymmetric risk" against the contestant. With this in mind, a player should choose "their case" and, as quickly as possible, discard 19 more cases until they are left with only six remaining. Any offer that is made up to that point should be answered by someone with their fingers plugging their ears, crying "LALALALA" at the top of their lungs. Why listen, since you know you shouldn't take the deal? This should be simple, right?

If it were that simple, the show "Deal or No Deal" would have been a flop. The math may be easy, but people are complex. What makes a good deal isn't simply the calculation of risk but also the calculation of reward. These things do not exist in a vacuum, so once again, we should consider looking at an example from the "inside out".

For a contestant facing a tough decision, many external factors would be identical for anyone standing in their shoes. They are standing on a stage in front of a studio audience. Lights are shining on them, and cameras are catching multiple angles of their every move. Their loved ones are shouting their advice, and the game show host is doing an excellent job at their assigned role of maximizing the drama of the situation. This is a television program and not the life of the contestant. Real life is what they will face when the cameras have stopped rolling and they have returned to their home, jobs, and bills.

Let's return to the example we started earlier. Once again, we have a contestant where a "fair deal" would entail an offer of $100,005. Let's assume that the offer made is to quit the game for $94,000. It's not a great deal by the numbers. But let's set math aside and focus on the person making the choice. This will be a brief study in the concept of making decisions from the inside out.

If we ignore all of the outside factors surrounding the production of a game show, we are left with only the contestant. What if she has a child with a chronic illness requiring a $75,000 medical procedure that her insurance doesn't cover? By numbers alone, the concept of symmetry says she should refuse the deal and keep playing with a potential upside of over $100,000 beyond the offer. The potential downside is only $94,000.

Considering the symmetry of her potential life outcomes changes the picture immensely. Taking the deal means that she will be guaranteed to have a healthy child and $19,000 left in the bank. This is an incredible outcome for having been chosen to participate in this game! Winning the highest prize still offers an upside of over $100,000 more, but only winning $10 means having to explain to a chronically sick child why they will not be receiving the necessary care. Suddenly, the downside seems far more serious than the upside. That's the power of asymmetric risk.

Risk Symmetry Grid – Example

	Best-Case Scenario	Worst-Case Scenario
What is the outcome?	Win $200,000	Win only $10
How likely is it?	50%	50%
How would it affect me?	Pay off debt, fund child's care	Cannot afford critical medical care

Game shows are constructed to build drama, and in our day-to-day lives, decisions aren't likely to have such high stakes. On the topic of risk symmetry, few places offer better examples than casinos. Consider the math behind a single roulette bet. If a person bets $100 on black, the worst they can do is lose their money. The best result that they can hope for is to win $100. The upside and downside are perfectly symmetrical. Can we say the same thing about the odds of winning? An American roulette wheel has 38 numbered slots. There are 18 red numbers, 18 black numbers, and two green numbers (0 and 00). The likelihood that your bet on black will win is 18/38 or 47.368%. This makes the odds of losing 52.632%. The odds are asymmetric, and they aren't in your favor.

If you were to look at round numbers, this might look like roughly 50/50 odds, but that little difference is all a casino needs to make millions of dollars. After all, Las Vegas was built entirely on the money of players who either didn't understand the math or chose to ignore it. Even if it was a 50/50 chance of winning, there is one last bit of symmetry that should be considered. Much like with our "Deal or No Deal" example of the mother of an ill child, we need to consider the personal effect of the probable outcomes. In explaining why he does not gamble, the longtime Jeopardy host, the late Alex Trebek, explained:

"I don't gamble because winning a hundred dollars doesn't give me great pleasure, but losing a hundred dollars p***es me off!"

In his case, even if the odds were a true 50/50 like that of a coin flip, his emotional response to loss outweighed his excitement over winning, creating psychological asymmetry. That compels him to avoid making the bet.

CONCLUSION

In this chapter, we have discussed using the concept of risk symmetry to help in making difficult decisions. We used a few stories and a bit of math, but here's a simple tool anyone can use. This method involves asking oneself six questions:

Best Case

- What is the best possible outcome?
- How likely is it?
- How would it affect me?

Worst Case

- What is the worst possible outcome?
- How likely is it?
- How would it affect me?

Consider these answers in pairs (1&4, 2&5, 3&6) and consider whether the outcomes are symmetrical. Let the asymmetrical outcomes be your guide as you consider what action to take.

TOOLS FOR YOUR KIT

KEY INSIGHT: Fairness isn't always in the odds; it's in the impact. A decision that looks balanced on paper may be deeply tilted once your personal risks are factored in.

MENTAL REFRAME: Smart decisions aren't just about winning; they're about avoiding outcomes you can't afford. Asymmetric risk means one side of the bet could ruin you, even if the odds look okay.

PRACTICAL TOOL: Use a 3-Lens Risk Filter before deciding:

1. Math: What are the actual probabilities? What's the expected value (gain × odds)?
2. Asymmetry: Is the downside far worse than the upside is good?
3. Personal Context: Would this outcome hurt you more than it would hurt someone else?

ACTION STEP: Pick a current risk you're evaluating. Fill out a quick version of this checklist:

- Likely Outcome
- Best Case
- Worst Case
- Can I live with the worst case?

If you can't tolerate the worst-case scenario, the decision may not be "fair" for you, no matter the stats.

BONUS TOOL: Look for low-downside, high-upside bets in life, where the worst-case scenario is manageable and the best-case scenario is transformative. That's how you stack the odds over time.

CHAPTER 8

BUSINESS AND CAREER DECISIONS:
THE CEO OF YOU

"I'm not a businessman, I'm a business, man."
—JAY-Z—

One of the biggest life-changing decisions is whether to become an entrepreneur. Entrepreneurs are often idolized today, though that hasn't always been the case, and may not last. The decision to work for oneself is filled with risks but can also bring incredible rewards. This chapter won't cover it all, but I'll share tools useful whether you're an employee or an entrepreneur.

Several decades ago, a university professor shared a perspective that has stayed with me throughout my career. This idea was relevant when I worked for a Fortune 500 company, sought employment with other businesses, and when I was self-employed. He argued that everyone is running a small business, even if it's just you selling your time and talent as an employee. You are in the business of being yourself. You develop your own culture, market yourself daily both inside and outside your company, manage your profits and losses, and invest in your growth.

How should you embrace and benefit from this mindset? Start by creating a business plan for yourself. You aren't necessarily trying to impress an angel investor or banker, so your plan doesn't need to be too well-polished. This is for you. Set goals. Build a strategic plan. That might mean learning new skills, growing your network, or tackling tough projects. Like a business owner, regularly assess your progress and adjust your strategies to stay on course towards your goals.

Next, put on the hat of your own chief marketing officer. Consider cultivating a personal brand. Just as businesses create a distinct identity to differentiate themselves from competitors, you should develop a unique professional identity. It's how you present yourself, communicate, and show your value. Consistently showcase your strengths and achievements, both in person and through online platforms like LinkedIn. In larger companies, you might benchmark against those above you. Your manager notices whose car is already in the parking lot and who stays late. They notice who volunteers, who dresses the part, and who steps up. Working through lunch or taking extra projects shows work ethic, and it gets noticed. When promotion time comes, perception matters. Sometimes it's as simple as who already looks the part. All of these areas and more can add up to your personal marketing strategy. Building a strong personal brand will make you more memorable and attractive to potential employers and clients alike.

> *"You, too, are a brand.*
> *Whether you know it or not.*
> *Whether you like it or not."*
> *— Mark Ecko*

Now become your own CFO (Chief Financial Officer), the one who watches the bottom line. Financial management is another crucial aspect of ensuring that the "business of you" is successful. Monitor your income and expenses carefully, as you would in a business. Create a budget that allows for both short-term costs like essential living expenses as well as future growth investments in your professional development, such as courses or conferences. Saving and investing wisely can provide a safety net during uncertain times and enable you to seize new opportunities without financial stress. We will pause with just a mention of personal finance in this chapter since we dedicate a great deal more time and content to the topic later.

As CEO of your one-person enterprise, you must also take ownership of the less concrete parts of your business plan. Networking drives business and your career. Consistent effort should be put into building and maintaining relationships with colleagues, mentors, and industry professionals. Some ways to extend your professional network quickly are attending industry events, joining professional associations, and perhaps participating in online communities relevant to your field. The combined effect of this collection of activities may not only lead to countless new opportunities but also provide several sources of insight and support.

Like a company building shareholder value, you should be building your own value every day. Stay current with industry trends, seek feedback, and be open to learning from both successes and failures. Dedicate part of every week towards expanding your knowledge base of your chosen field. Find like-minded people with whom you can engage in meaningful conversations about the business landscape, as well as your professional futures. Like any successful business, realizing your best possible professional future requires continuous improvement, education, and adaptation.

By using the tools of a small business owner, even if you technically are not one, you take control of your career. This means planning ahead and making deliberate choices that align with your goals and values. This proactive approach can bring you greater job satisfaction, career advancement, and ultimately, more fulfillment in many areas of your life.

To Commute or Not to Commute

Many stops along my own career journey involved a great deal of travel. Some years, this involved a total number of flights in the triple digits. If someone were to add up the number of nights that I have slept in hotel beds, the sum would be measured in years (yes...plural)! Before I was a professional "road warrior," I still engaged in some business travel but more often could be found spending my work hours sitting in offices and cubicles. While these types of work environments still exist, the post-Covid era has created a noted increase in telecommuting positions, hybrid roles, and entire organizations with nothing but remote employees. At some point, you'll have to decide: office or remote? It's not one-size-fits-all, and the answer depends on many factors.

Career Advancement and Networking

Getting back to the value of one's network, some connections are built only in person, through mentorships, collaboration, or casual hallway chats. This may take the form of something as influential as a mentorship relationship or simply spontaneous, casual interactions that generate great ideas. We should also not overlook the importance of office friendships as they have the potential to improve our everyday lives over the short and long terms.

In the interest of balance, we should consider the symmetry that may or may not exist when it comes to the pros and cons of sharing physical space with one's professional colleagues. Office politics can easily create distractions from important work or, worse yet, may cause uncomfortable or stressful situations.

Work-Life Considerations

There are undeniable benefits to working remotely. Doing so often permits a person to have a more flexible work schedule, allowing them to commit more time and energy during a "traditional work week" to family and personal commitments. Some people can't stand commuting, and the avoidance of that can save them from a daily source of stress. Beyond avoiding a negative, there is the added benefit of having a bit more time in the day to dedicate to personal wellness activities like exercise, reading, or meditation.

Of course, from the perspective of work-life balance, working remotely doesn't come with only benefits. There are downsides too, like isolation, or the blurred line between work and home. For many, after our college years, the workplace can provide an important source of social interactions. While letting one's profession be a source of some personal friendships may be a plus, there are potential negative side effects of working from home that stem from blurring the line between the personal and the professional. Some people struggle to "disconnect" from the workplace when they have constant access to all of the tools of their profession in a home office. Such difficulty in setting and maintaining boundaries can lead to potential burnout or take a serious toll on one's relationships with loved ones within the household.

Your Work Style

A little self-awareness may go a long way toward determining if a remote work arrangement is right for you. Do you seek collaboration or work better independently? How do you handle distractions from coworkers? Is your job role one that primarily requires digital communication and limited physical presence? While being off-site may be fine for a data analyst, it would certainly be trickier for someone in the healthcare field.

The Economics of Remote Work

The last consideration we will discuss regarding the decision to work remotely is the bottom line: money. The savings that come from eliminating one's commute include fuel, insurance, and wear and tear on one's vehicle. For many, the commute comes with the added cost of the irresistible allure of your favorite coffee shop en route. It all adds up. Beyond coffee and a bagel, going to the office also increases your odds of going out to eat lunch more often or hitting happy hour after quitting time. It's not hard to see how one's total expenses can be greatly affected by staying home. The purchase and maintenance of professional attire also add to the total cost of the office lifestyle.

Depending on the employer, you may be able to work at an unlimited distance from any office location. This would grant you the ability to live in a lower-cost area of the country, cutting down on any number of household expenses from housing to groceries. Keep in mind that some employers may adjust salaries based on the cost of living associated with where an employee chooses to live.

Some areas where it may save money to stay close to the office are related more to one's activities outside of work/working hours. If you require child care, a large employer may provide a low-cost on-site option. Many large workplaces have facilities like on-site fitness centers or health and wellness programs. These may be provided as low-cost or no-cost benefits to local employees. Lastly, some employers provide opportunities for cost-effective recreation. These may range from company tickets to a concert or athletic event to participation in a corporate sports league. For the right employee, these could contribute meaningfully to lowering household expenses.

WHO YOU KNOW AND WHAT THEY SAY

"Your network is your net worth."
— Tim Sanders

As mentioned above, if done correctly, traveling the road toward your best possible future will involve the intersections of many others. While I strongly encourage engaging with numerous people in your field or simply the world at large...I do so with a word of caution.

Everyone loves to give advice. I guess it's only human. After all, it feels good to be acknowledged as the sage giver of wisdom. Perhaps this is one area where human nature serves us well: it is pleasurable to do something so generous as to offer the benefit of our thoughts and experiences to someone else. (In a moment of introspection, I can't help but wonder if that is why I am writing this book.) Since advice is free and potentially quite beneficial, I can wholeheartedly suggest that you collect as much as you can. Returning to a prior chapter's concept of asymmetric risk, we can say that the upside of getting good advice is clear, and the downside is almost nonexistent. This is true so long as you remember one caveat: there is no risk in collecting all the advice you can, but there is a great risk in following it. Not all advice is created equal.

My mother is long-retired from a 25-year career working in real estate. I have bought and sold several homes in my adult life and consulted with her on every transaction. Once, I even asked her to travel from her home in Florida to the Atlanta area to assist me in selling a house there. She knows more about residential real estate than I ever will (or intend to). This having been established, many of my best choices in other areas of life have been in direct opposition to Mom's advice. Of course, she wants what is best for me, but that doesn't change the fact that she is not a good source of guidance in all areas.

When I left my first job with a Fortune 100 company, Mom thought I had lost my mind. My parents were from a generation when it was common for a person to work their entire career for one employer, like my father had for over thirty years. Job security was of great importance to them, particularly since my parents were providing for a family of six by the time they were both 30 years old. In hindsight, this career decision unlocked a world of possibilities for me and was a critical early step to a much brighter future. Despite her best intentions, Mom's advice came from a place where her lived experience conflicted with what would have been the best guidance for me. When I entered the world of entrepreneurship, I continued to receive my mother's best advice but found myself following it less and less, understanding that she had never owned and operated a small business.

Returning to the secret of receiving advice: the reason all advice is not created equal is that all advice givers are not the same. We need a system for evaluating each one for their level of followability.

Scoring "Followability" of an Advice-Giver

Receiving the most benefit from the collective knowledge of the people you encounter requires you to have a method for knowing whose opinions are the most useful. Today, it is important to be able to evaluate both those who give out advice to the masses through traditional media or online, as well as those who you may encounter in your day-to-day life. Here are some useful criteria for considering individual pieces of advice and the situational value of those who gave it.

Qualifications

Modern technology allows us to rather quickly and easily obtain information about a few specific areas of a person's qualifications in a particular area. Looking up someone's educational background can inform you what degrees they have obtained and what institutions they attended while completing their academic achievements.

Beyond one's education, we would consider whether or not their professional experience makes them more or less qualified to give good advice on a specific topic. Some simple Q&A or a bit of online research can help uncover information on the professional positions that a person has held, as well as how long they were in each position. A little more digging should help you learn how much the duties performed yielded experience that can be considered relevant to your specific situation.

Research and Recognition

There are several ways that someone can establish themselves as a valued resource on a specific topic. In an academic setting, this can be accomplished by publishing research. Other ways to have one's thoughts published are articles and books. Once someone's thoughts and opinions have been published, a quick internet search can tell you how often their ideas have been cited by others. This is one way to gauge their impact on a specific area.

As print becomes a progressively less important form of communication, it may also make sense to research a person's online presence. Can you read any past issues of an electronic newsletter or blog? Are there videos available of this person speaking on a topic about your specific decision? What can you learn from their social media presence? What success stories have been shared?

Someone's reputation in a specific field can also, in part, be measured by recognitions beyond citations in print or digital media. Are they the recipient of any prestigious awards? Have their peers granted them membership in any professional associations? Has anyone you know and trust recommended this person for their expertise or otherwise offered their endorsement?

A Final Word on Receiving Someone's Advice

Now that you've evaluated this person's level of qualifications for advising on a topic, you should remember to take a moment to remember that they are only human. Just because they can give good advice does not necessarily mean that they do so every time. I suggest revisiting a quick list of the biases that we covered earlier in this book and ask yourself if this person could be falling victim to any of these:

- **Anchoring** - using an irrelevant reference point for making decisions
- **Confirmation Bias** - tending to notice things that support an existing belief
- **Groupthink** - failing to consider a decision in order to get along fully
- **Self-Interest Bias** - favoring information that benefits someone personally
- **The Affect Heuristic** - relying on emotional responses to make judgments
- **Saliency Bias** - focusing on information that is most easily noticeable
- **Availability Bias** - relying on the most available information
- **Halo Effect** - Letting positive traits lead to an overall judgment

CONCLUSION

Making thoughtful decisions in your career and business is crucial for long-term success and fulfillment. I fully support the approach of treating your career like you are running your own small business, even if you are not. This means setting clear goals, engaging in strategic planning, and regularly assessing your progress. Whether you're aiming for a promotion, considering a career change, or thinking about starting your own business, having a solid plan can guide your decisions and keep you on track.

Financial management is critical for both career and business success. Monitor your income and expenses carefully, budget for both immediate needs and long-term investments, and save for future opportunities or challenges. This financial discipline provides a safety net and allows you to take advantage of new opportunities without unnecessary stress.

Personal branding is another essential aspect of career management. Present yourself consistently and authentically, both in person and online, to showcase your unique strengths and achievements. By building a strong personal brand, you make yourself more memorable and attractive to potential employers or clients. Networking also plays a vital role; maintaining professional relationships can open doors to new opportunities and provide valuable support and insights.

Whether they know it or not, consider your professional influences to be informal members of your board of directors. Take in as much information and as many opinions as you can, but always evaluate them for quality and believability.

Consider where your "headquarters" should be. There are many issues to consider with regard to everything from expenses to quality of life.

Finally, continuous learning and improvement are vital. Stay updated with industry trends, seek feedback, and learn from your successes and failures. Dedicate time to expanding your knowledge and skills, and engage with others in your field to discuss developments and future possibilities. By approaching your career with this proactive, business-minded attitude, you can achieve greater satisfaction, success, and fulfillment.

TOOLS FOR YOUR KIT

KEY INSIGHT: You are the CEO of the Business of You. No one will care about your trajectory more than you do, so you need to lead, strategize, and invest accordingly.

MENTAL REFRAME: Your career isn't a ladder. It's a company with assets, partnerships, marketing, finances, and growth strategies. Treat it like one.

PRACTICAL TOOL: Run a Personal Annual Review as if you're managing a business:

- **Strategy:** What are your 1-year and 5-year goals?
- **Marketing:** How are you showcasing your skills and story? (LinkedIn, portfolio, referrals)
- **Finance:** Track your income, expenses, savings rate, and how much you're investing in your development.
- **Operations:** Are you working in a way that aligns with your energy, boundaries, and long-term growth?

Curate a Board of Directors:

- Include mentors, colleagues, and trusted peers
- Listen widely, but filter wisely
- Always check for bias, relevance, and intent

ACTION STEP: Make a one-page "Business of Me" snapshot:

- Mission Statement
- Current Position (income, role, skills)
- Top 3 Areas for Growth
- One Big Goal for the next 12 months

BONUS TOOL: Evaluate your work environment like a CFO. Remote vs. in-office isn't just preference; it's a productivity, mental health, and growth equation. Know your ideal conditions, and advocate for them.

CHAPTER 9

DECISION FATIGUE:
WHY WILLPOWER ISN'T ENOUGH

TO SAY IT WAS A LONG DAY would be an understatement. It was one of those days that drains your energy and your ability to make good decisions. It began with a two-hour drive to a place most people dread: a car dealership. The stats back this up. A 2024 survey by the analytics firm KPA shows why Americans dread the car lot. Seventy-six percent of the respondents indicated that they don't trust dealerships regarding pricing. An even greater 86% revealed that they had concerns about hidden fees. In the end, 29% of the over 2000 people who took the survey actually left the dealership because they sensed dishonesty. On this particular day, my wife and I would have been among that 29%, but it wasn't necessarily easy to walk away.

My bride wanted a very specific vehicle, and after extensive searching, we found the nearest dealer for her specific vehicle a few counties away. Given the long round-trip, I spent hours emailing and calling to iron out every detail beforehand. I did not want to waste a trip. Before we started our drive, I knew the exact car we were going to buy and the price, and I even had the name of the salesperson who had corresponded with me several times via email. I imagined that all we had to do was make sure that we received a fair offer for our trade-in and that Amy enjoyed her test drive.

When we arrived, we entered the showroom, and a salesperson came to greet us. This wasn't the person from the emails, as we were told he was busy working with other buyers. We handed over the keys to our trade-in so that they could inspect it. We also provided my wife's driver's license so they could hold onto it during the test drive, which went wonderfully. She loved the car, unfortunately.

The troubles started when the salesperson refused to honor the price we discussed via e-mail. I got visibly annoyed and simply refused to continue a discussion with someone who I thought was engaging in dishonest behavior. They sent over another salesperson who similarly would not honor that price. A great deal of time later, yet another salesperson explained to us that even their printed advertisement in that weekend's newspaper was not a number that they could work with. After over five hours of "negotiation" with four different sales representatives, we decided we had had enough and told them we were leaving. We were wrong. We had forgotten that we had given them Amy's license and the keys to her car several hours earlier. These items had apparently been "misplaced" in the meantime, which coincidentally provided enough time for them to send over one more salesperson to try to close the deal while they "searched" for the missing items.

In the end, we did leave that dealership and bought a different vehicle at another dealership down the street. They had a "no haggle" policy, and we were driving off in my wife's new car (which she still loves) about one hour later. I had wasted weeks of research and correspondence, as well as hours of dealing with the first dealership, but the final result was good. There was a question eating at me, though. How did the first company blow such an easy sale?! After all, we walked into their door that afternoon with every intention of paying them an agreed-upon price for a specific vehicle.

The answer to that question appears to be two-fold. Of course, the obvious explanation is simple greed. They knew they had a very interested buyer. After all, who would put in weeks of telephone and email negotiations, hours of driving, and even more hours of negotiation to walk away empty-handed? They thought they had enough leverage to squeeze us for more money. The second reason they thought they would win is a bit more complicated.

In their research for "Order in Product Customization Decisions," Professors Jonathan Levav, Mark Heitmann, Andreas Herrmann, and Sheena S. Iyengar uncovered an inconvenient truth. Their study revealed a troubling link between fatigue and overspending. Their study was of customers in German automobile dealerships. The subjects were real purchasers spending their own hard-earned money. Buyers started by carefully weighing options, but as time wore on, that changed. As fatigue set in, they were far more likely to simply settle for the path of least resistance. In the end, the diminished willpower of the subjects came at a cost. On average, fatigue cost each buyer an extra $2,000.

With that in mind, our failed dealership trip makes more sense. After five hours of exhausting discussions, we would very likely be fatigued. By swapping out salespeople every hour or so, the dealership would be less likely to have this problem. They could reasonably expect that we would settle for the easiest path forward, even at our own expense. Scientific study, and no doubt experience, had taught them that this was a likely outcome. They were wrong in this case, but I suspect it may have been an exception to the rule.

SAME PHENOMENON, MUCH HIGHER PRICE

While a couple of thousand dollars is no small thing, another study showed that this type of mental exhaustion has caused others to pay a much higher price. The research of Jonathan Levav and Shai Danziger concluded that simple fatigue has literally cost some men their very freedom. They found that the biggest factor in whether an inmate received parole was something completely out of their control. Regardless of factors like the nature of their crimes, the length of their sentence, or even their ethnicity, the outcome of a parole hearing was largely a function of the time of day that the meeting took place.

Before you ask, the study was not on a small number of cases. The researchers analyzed more than 1,100 decisions over a year. You might suspect that the relationship between being granted parole and the time of your hearing was loose and therefore potentially misinterpreted. The fact is that prisoners who faced the parole board in the early morning were successful about 70 percent of the time. Those who were seen late in the day were granted parole less than 10 percent of the time!

DECISION FATIGUE

In psychology, "decision fatigue" is the mental wear that weakens our choices after a long decision-making session. To put it more simply, making good decisions is exhausting. The more exhausted your decision-making systems become, the worse your decisions will be. This is not new information to those who stand to benefit from your bad decisions. That's why candy lives by the checkout lane. After the countless choices you've made while navigating the store aisles (not to mention anything else that day), they hope that you simply won't have the emotional strength remaining to say no to that chocolate bar.

There are several ways to combat decision fatigue. Here is one:

Fewer Decisions = Better Decisions

The more decisions you make, the worse your decisions get. So: make fewer of them. Fewer decisions means a higher average quality of decision. If this is the case, there is a clear benefit to treating each good decision as something of great value and a finite supply. Treat your decision-making capacity as limited. Don't waste it!

PRE-DECIDING THE UNIMPORTANT:
A CASE STUDY

Many successful people across such diverse fields as business, politics, and the arts provide evidence of the benefits of reducing "decision waste". The image below is a sample of the results from a Google image search of the term "Barack Obama."

The two-term president of the United States eliminated one simple decision from almost every workday. He decided to waste almost none of his mental capacity on the "what to wear" decision. He did this by narrowing his options to two or three variations of a dark suit jacket, a blue or grey tie, and a light shirt. By keeping to this "uniform", he may have given himself the ability to make one more good decision each day! For other examples of this method of fending off decision fatigue, one could look at the black turtleneck and jeans of the late Apple CEO Steve Jobs or the daily grey t-shirt of Facebook's Mark Zuckerberg.

What other decisions can you cut out of your daily routine? Can you eat the same thing for breakfast, or at least slim down your menu? Can you stick to more of a routine in order to reduce the number of times you have to ask yourself, "What do I do next?" Examine your daily life for decisions of little consequence. Ask yourself if each one is worth spending energy on every day or if you should just decide once and live by your decision.

LET SOMEONE ELSE DECIDE

Every time I get a haircut in a new place, they ask the same thing: "What do you want to do with it?" I always give them the same response: "You are the professional. I trust that you know more about what looks good than I do." I mean this when I say it. I do not live in a world where I spend a great deal of time and energy thinking about what hairstyles are fashionable. I don't know what hair products to buy or how to apply them. Who am I to tell a hair expert what to do with a head of hair? This person went to school to learn this skill, got licensed, bought the tools, and worked on hair 40 hours a week.

Haircuts are low-stakes, but trusting an expert frees up your energy for higher-stakes decisions. Preserve your decision-making abilities so that you can apply them to the areas where YOU are the expert. Trusting other experts saves your decision power for where it matters most.

In this way, we can all benefit. The hairstylist makes my decision so that I can make a better investment decision for a doctor, who in turn makes a better medical decision for a police officer... and the chain reaction of better decision-making continues.

ONE MORE TRICK

What if, in part, the solution was hiding in the problem? Earlier in this chapter I mentioned the cost of decision fatigue when faced with the impulse snacks in the checkout aisle of your local grocery store. A study by social psychologist Roy F. Baumeister found that resisting one temptation makes it harder to resist the next. Using our example from the snack aisle, the implication is that grabbing that candy bar may actually help you make your next decision a bit better. There is another reason why the stores are particularly successful at selling candy and soda to exhausted shoppers. Thinking burns energy, so your brain needs fuel to function. Specifically, it needs glucose. While this simple sugar is in all sorts of food, it is easy to see how an exhausted brain would quickly reach out for a particularly sweet snack or beverage to get that quick "sugar rush." The good news is that once you've potentially succumbed to a moment of weakness and eaten the candy, you likely have eased the effects of your depleting willpower. Not only that, but you may have temporarily reversed the effects of decision fatigue to the extent that you will be able to make improved choices for a little while longer. In Baumeister's study, people's self-control and the quality of their choices both improved measurably. When asked to make financial decisions, they proved to be more resistant to irrational bias and were more likely to choose a better long-term strategy over a shorter-term solution. Ironically, eating the candy bar, the very thing you were trying to resist, may restore your ability to make better decisions.

This area of study was continued by scientist Todd Heatherton, who wanted to know more about the specific ways that depleted energy affects willpower. Confirming the findings of the Baumeister study, his work determined that the brain doesn't just stop or slow down when low on glucose. It responds more to immediate rewards and less to longer-term outcomes. Willpower doesn't just fade; it shifts your brain into short-term mode.

Connecting this information with our earlier study of the Israeli parole board, it is worth noting that a mid-morning snack made a noticeable difference in parole hearing outcomes. Not only was there a more than 60% increased chance of parole for earlier cases over later ones, but the people in the middle of the day could benefit from their timing relative to a break for the judges. If you were fortunate enough to appear in front of the panel after they ate some fruit and a sandwich each morning, your odds of parole were about 45% higher than someone who had their hearing just before snack time. A sandwich and some fruit didn't just boost energy; they changed lives.

CONCLUSION

Each of us can be a victim of decision fatigue. It is simply a function of biology. Accepting decision fatigue helps us design better days and smarter lives, where we make fewer, smarter choices. We can optimize the number of big decisions that we make when we are at our highest ability to do so well. We can avoid scheduling long sessions of uninterrupted decision-making. We can limit the number of relatively inconsequential decisions that we make, and we can endeavor to maintain proper nutrition to avoid diminished willpower and a potential inclination toward short-term thinking to the detriment of our long-term well-being. A little foresight and thoughtful structuring of our time can help us avoid having to rely on the inherently fluctuating reservoir of willpower. Plan your day, not your willpower.

TOOLS FOR YOUR KIT

KEY INSIGHT: Good decisions don't just come from willpower; they come from energy management. If you want better outcomes, protect your bandwidth.

MENTAL REFRAME: You don't need to be superhuman; you need to be strategic. Decision-making is a finite resource. Spend it wisely.

PRACTICAL TOOL: Use The Four R's to manage decision fatigue:

- **Reduce:** Eliminate or delegate low-impact decisions
- **Rest:** Take intentional mental breaks. Don't stack hard choices back-to-back
- **Routine:** Automate the basics (meals, clothes, commute) to save bandwidth
- **Refuel:** Don't make big calls when you're hungry, dehydrated, or drained

ACTION STEP: Schedule your next big decision for your personal peak time (e.g., morning if that's when you're sharpest). Block 30–60 minutes, free from distractions, and come prepared with a snack and water.

BONUS TOOL: If a decision feels stuck, try the Walk + Reset Method:

- Step away for 15–30 minutes
- Walk, breathe, or shift focus
- Return with a fresh brain, and often, a clearer path

CHAPTER 10

FINANCES:
REAL ADVICE FOR REAL WEALTH

THERE ARE THOUSANDS OF BOOKS on personal finance. Considering my career, I might write one someday. This is NOT that book. But since this book is about big decisions, it would be a huge oversight not to include financial ones.

Since I work in finance and investments, a quick disclaimer is in order. Nothing you will read in this book should be considered investment, tax, or legal "advice". To give you any of those, I would need to know a great deal more about you than the simple fact that you have great taste in books. Giving financial advice without real knowledge of a person and their specific situation would be terribly irresponsible, if not dangerous. (Now my attorneys and regulators can sleep a bit better tonight).

This brings us to my first piece of guidance: choose your financial sources carefully.

WHO IS WORTH LISTENING TO ABOUT YOUR MONEY?

In the chapter on Business and Career Decisions, we developed a checklist for evaluating the "followability" of an advice-giver. In finance, there are a few extra red flags to watch for beyond credentials and bias. These fall into three main categories: protection, compensation, and motivation.

Protections

There are systems in place to protect the public financially. The first concept that comes to mind is FDIC insurance. This exists to protect the deposits of bank customers, up to certain limits, at member banks. It's often the first financial protection people encounter. Beyond bank deposits, things get a bit more complicated. Some guarantees aren't backed by the FDIC, and not all guarantees are created equal. A question worth asking about any guarantee is, "Who is making it?". Also ask: how do they plan to back it up? During the Great Recession, many annuity investors learned hard lessons about the guarantees backed by some life insurance companies. While being backed by the "full faith and credit of WXYZ Corporation" may give us a sense of security, it is only useful as long as WXYZ is in a solid enough financial condition to pay off all of its obligations. It's easy to see how a guarantee like this could seem considerably less valuable than one backed by the full faith and credit of the taxing authority of the United States of America, as one would find with a U.S. Treasury Bond. Investment products can be guaranteed by a variety of private and public entities. These entities can secure these guarantees with specific revenue sources or as a general obligation. All of these factors influence the value of a guarantee and should be understood before committing one's funds.

Another structure that protects investors is that of a standard of care. There's a long-running battle over enforcing the fiduciary standard in finance. This standard requires financial professionals to act in their clients' best interests. They must act prudently, avoiding any conflicts of interest. While there are many advisors today that must adhere to this standard, there are many more that are not required to do so. A "suitability standard" is less stringent and allows for recommendations that may be more costly and/or generate higher commissions for the financial professional. The suitability standard is used by many broker-dealer firms and their affiliates. My simple guidance on this topic is to ask two questions to any investment professional:

1. Are you held to a fiduciary standard of care?
2. Are there any times when you are not?

Compensation

Related to the concept of standard of care is the question of compensation. It is fair to assess a person's believability if you know that your decision directly affects their income! The personal finance industry has historically been quite creative when it comes to inventing ways to get paid. Even today, one major American brokerage firm publishes a PDF entitled "Understanding how we are compensated for financial services," which is 46 pages long! This is a company with over 19,000 employees working in over 15,000 offices throughout North America. Clients of a company like this could be paying commissions, mark-ups, administrative fees, margin fees, and numerous other items contributing to a broker's compensation and the bottom line of the corporation. My basic guidance on this topic is once again to ask a direct question. I encourage you to ask any financial professional that you are considering hiring to list all of the ways that they and their employers are compensated. Listen for an answer that is short and easy to understand. Exercise extreme caution if you feel yourself becoming confused or overwhelmed during their reply. If your advisor's pay structure requires a 46-page explanation... that's a red flag.

What Is True Motivation?

This one's tricky; it may make you rethink even your favorite financial voices. You may listen to a very popular radio show on finances or watch a cable television program about trading stocks. There are many of both. The thing you must keep in mind is the motivation of the talking head on the other side of your TV or Radio. Their true "job" is to sell advertising. It is NOT to give good financial advice. The problem? Good advice is often boring. These are concepts like "pay down your high-interest debt" and "spend less than you earn." The problem with these boring but effective notions is that they do not keep people glued to their devices for a full hour, forcing them to take in a few commercials every so often. Those ad dollars pay the host, the studio, and the entire crew. Today, I suppose that it is every bit as important to offer a similar warning about the "financial influencers" on social media. People have become millionaires by giving questionable financial guidance on platforms like YouTube, Instagram, and TikTok. If the fortunes lost in cryptocurrencies, meme stocks, and NFTs taught us two things, it is that the influencers do not care about you, and they are not in the business of giving prudent advice. They're not in the business of giving you good advice. They're in the business of keeping your attention. After all, more "watch time" ensures that you will see a few more advertisements. Just like on TV and Radio, advertising dollars are the lifeblood of the social media economy.

Once we get away from the professional media hosts, we should still examine the motivation of those whom we might more reasonably expect to be motivated to truly help. In recent years, there have been a few new entrants into the universe of investment platforms. One appealing feature that some of the most popular ones had in common was that they were presented as "free" to use. A popular mobile application, named Robinhood, known for "zero-commission stock trading," was forced to pay a multimillion-dollar settlement to the United States Securities and Exchange Commission for the failure to disclose a system of kickbacks to institutional market participants. The money that Robinhood collected from these "market makers" came at an invisible cost to their customers insofar as Robinhood failed to ensure that investors were receiving the best prices on their orders. They were making a substantial portion of the company's revenues by selling their clients' transactions in the form of "payment for order flow."

Robinhood investors thought they were customers benefiting from a free trading service. In truth, they were not the customer, but rather the product being sold to an invisible group of buyers.

Now that we've covered who to trust, let's talk about two broad principles that can help anyone make better financial decisions.

TWO BROAD TENETS

Tenet #1:
Your Wealth is a Function of the Money
You Haven't Spent

Theodore Roosevelt once said, "Comparison is the thief of joy." If this was true in Teddy's day, I can't help but wonder what he would think of our modern version of "keeping up with the Joneses." It was bad enough when grocery store tabloids and Robin Leach provided occasional looks into the lifestyles of the rich and famous. Today, we have 24-hour reality TV networks and numerous social media outlets showing a nonstop, touched-up, fantasy version of your closest friends' day-to-day lives. It has gotten easier and easier to fall into the trap of feeling like everyone you know is doing better than you are.

Keeping up with the Joneses in this day and age has measurable effects on society. People who bought houses they could not afford contributed to the housing bubble that peaked less than 20 years ago. Every year, more and more people choose to lease expensive luxury cars or commit to longer and longer auto loans in order to be seen driving something that may be beyond their true financial means.

If the Joneses represent what is typical in American society, we should take a closer look at what typical means. The most recent Federal Reserve report on the Economic Well-Being of US Households sheds a startling light on what it means to be the average American household. The study found that nearly half of respondents could not cover an emergency expense costing $400 or would have to raise the money by selling something or borrowing. Almost half of non-retirees in the study with self-directed retirement accounts were either "not confident" or only "slightly confident" in their ability to make the right investment decisions. These examples are only the tip of a disconcerting iceberg.

It is easy to fall into the trap of trying to keep up with the Joneses. For many, this leads to living right up to or beyond the ceiling of what their income will allow. A certain "lifestyle inflation" may have taken hold when your saving habits are shrinking or your debt is growing, just so you can be proud of having the latest version of your smartphone.

I have the privilege of working with some very extraordinary and successful individuals, and my time around them has come with a free education of sorts. One important lesson learned is this:

If you do what everyone else does, you can only have the life that everyone else has.

Don't be like the nearly half of Americans who can't afford a $400 emergency. Start saving up an emergency fund! Don't be like the nervous half of non-retirees in self-directed retirement accounts. Go get some direction from a professional! Don't live beyond your means. Don't try to keep up with the Joneses. The Joneses are broke!

The mistake that the Joneses made is believing that the stuff they bought is the measure of their wealth, but they have it almost exactly backward. The most dangerous form of comparison is the one that we don't realize is happening. We don't see what people didn't buy; we only see what they did. Your true wealth is made up of the money that you haven't spent. It is this money that grants you the freedom to seize opportunities. It is this money that allows you to sleep soundly at night, knowing that you are financially bulletproof and that a small emergency will not throw your entire life out of balance. Rather than spending on visible objects to impress other people, the truly wealthy first save for the invisible sense of financial well-being.

Tenet #2:
You Can Have Anything,
Just Not Everything Right Now

(There is a way to get everything you want, though.)

Everyone has a list (mental or otherwise) of desires. I suspect that on some level, many people believe that their happiness depends on having what they want. I will save the discussion on the validity of that belief for another day. For now, let's just assume that it is true. The interesting thing is that having everything that you want is a shockingly simple thing to achieve. I will approach this solution using some simple mathematics.

Let's assume that if what a person has (H) is greater than or equal to what a person wants (W) then they will be happy.

Or $H \geq W$ = 😊 .

How are we to achieve this condition? The obvious method is through the attainment of the list of things you want (increasing the value of H). This is simply a matter of paying the price for those things you want, thereby converting them into things you have. To quote the book, Walden:

> *"The cost of a thing is the amount of what I will call life which is required to be exchanged for it, immediately or in the long run."*
> —Henry David Thoreau

So long as you are willing to do what it takes (by trading your time, energy, and resources) to get the things on your list, you can have them. The problem here is that the cost may be high, the work may be difficult, and the process may take a very long time. Thankfully, there is a second method to having everything that you want.

If we return to the idea that H must be greater than or equal to W, then the second way to achieve this should be obvious. Instead of paying the price to obtain more "haves" (increasing the value of H), you can simply endeavor to want less (reducing the value of W).

I may have promised a simple solution, but I never claimed that it would necessarily be easy. Reducing your W will likely involve examining your priorities ("How important is this to me really?") and your

motivations ("Why do I want this? Is it to impress the neighbors?").
To return to pages of Walden:

> *"A man is rich in proportion to the number of things*
> *which he can afford to let alone."*
> *—Henry David Thoreau*

While I have a definite admiration for those who lead a happy life of
few and simple needs, I do not want to overlook the benefits of paying
the price for more when it makes sense. I believe that there are things
in everyone's life for which it is worth "paying the price". The good
news is that one does not have to choose between the solutions of
having more and wanting less. There is no doubt a certain balance and
equilibrium to creating the vision of one's ideal life and doing what it
takes to make it a reality. I can't help but throw in one last bit of Walden wisdom:

> *"If you have built castles in the air, your work need not be lost; that is where*
> *they should be. Now put the foundations under them."*
> *—Henry David Thoreau*

You don't have to give up on your dreams, but you'll likely have to do
the work to build under them. To put this into a step-by-step structure,
I give you the following:

- Make a list of everything you want.
- Forget about the things that you can "afford to let alone"
- Determine the cost (be it time, money, or effort) of having the
  things that are left.
- Get to work

TOOLS FOR YOUR KIT

🔑 **KEY INSIGHT:** Wealth isn't just about what you earn; it's about what you keep. And the advice you follow should serve you, not the interests of someone else.

💿 **MENTAL REFRAME:** Rich isn't a number. It's freedom from needing more. You can have everything you want if you either want less, or earn more intentionally.

🔧 **PRACTICAL TOOL:** RUN all advice-givers through a Three-Filter Test:

1. **Structural**: Is this person legally or ethically obligated to act in your best interest?
2. **Financial**: How are they getting paid? Do they benefit from your decision?
3. **Motivational**: What's driving them: your outcome, their ego, or their paycheck?

Then revisit your Wealth Equation: Income – Unnecessary Spending = Wealth

Protect your unspent money as a limited resource. It's your future options fund.

✅ **ACTION STEP:** Write down 3 recurring expenses you could eliminate this month without losing quality of life. Then write one thing you'd invest in instead, something that grows your freedom, not just your lifestyle.

🎺 **BONUS TOOL:** Consider Thoreau's perspective: "A man is rich in proportion to the number of things which he can afford to let alone." True wealth is peace with enough.

CHAPTER 11

MARSHMALLOWS AND
TIME MACHINES:
LOOK INTO YOUR FUTURE

IN 1970, Stanford psychologist Walter Mischel conducted a now-famous experiment with 32 children aged three to five. Researchers followed the children for years and discovered that a single choice during the experiment predicted future outcomes with surprising accuracy. These measurements included Scholastic Aptitude Test (SAT) Scores and health outcomes (as measured by body mass index (BMI), as well as some other criteria. What was the one decision that was so powerful in predicting the future of a small child? It was when to eat a marshmallow.

In the original experiment, and several that followed, the children were led into a room, where they chose a snack. The 1972 study conducted by Mischel, Ebbesen, and Zeiss is today referred to as the "Stanford Marshmallow Experiment" since the reward used was a marshmallow. The treat was placed in front of the child, and the rules were clearly explained. The child was allowed to eat the treat; however, if the scientist returned to the room after 15 minutes to discover that the marshmallow had not been eaten, the reward would be doubled.

Children invented clever tricks to hold out for the bigger prize. Some covered their eyes, others sang songs or created games to play. One even managed to take a nap. The key to doubling their reward? The ability to ignore temptation, literally. In the end, the indicator of future success in many areas of life was the ability to delay immediate gratification. A 2011 brain imaging study revisited the original participants, now adults, and found lasting differences in brain activity. These differences appeared in two key brain regions, especially when participants were resisting temptation.

From experience, I can say that the rewards for delayed gratification grow as we get older. If three-year-olds are already wired to resist or give in to temptation, what chance do the rest of us have to outperform our biology? Those of us who are not hard-wired for such discipline could use some tools and tactics.

FIRE UP THE FLEX CAPACITOR

Hollywood often shows us what it's like to glimpse the future and see how today's choices play out. Whether it is George Bailey in *It's a Wonderful Life*, or Marty McFly in *Back to the Future*, the message is the same. Being able to glimpse the future can greatly improve the decisions we make in the present.

While we don't have working crystal balls or nuclear-powered Deloreans, it can be surprisingly simple to see into the future of some decisions. Unfortunately, the difficulty for many is making the best use of the information that is available. This can be especially true when it comes to decisions around delayed gratification. We know that heavy drinking usually leads to a hangover and a lighter wallet, and in this case, those are the mildest consequences one could face. What if we were living in an alternate version of Charles Dickens' *A Christmas Carol*, and just for a moment that night, we could have a quick conversation with 'The Ghost of a Hangover Yet to Come'? Even a glimpse a few hours ahead might be enough to say, "I've had enough," a few rounds earlier and save ourselves from the eventual pain. If the mental exercise of picturing your future self doesn't work this time, that person can help you avoid repeating a mistake next time. Perhaps write yourself a quick note when you are fully feeling the consequences of a poor decision. Put it in your wallet or purse as a reminder. Use the clarity of this tough moment to set personal policies for next time. Try leaving your credit card at home and using only a set amount of cash. Maybe a friend wants the same improvement and can be your accountability partner. You might even be able to enlist the services of a particularly ethical bartender in keeping you to a preset limit. These are just a few methods you could try employing to avoid making future predictably suboptimal choices.

Not all decisions have such foreseeable consequences, but there are certainly plenty that do. It is not difficult to look into the future and see what the effects would be of opting for the immediate gratification that may come from overeating or perhaps making an impulse purchase on one's credit card. When the outcomes are this obvious, take a moment to have a mental conversation with the future you who may be dealing with long-term health problems or buried under a mountain of high-interest debt.

On the topic of impulse purchases, there is one mental exercise that has successfully saved me plenty of my own money. This also involves an inevitable event in the future and a quick trip in our imaginary time machine. It is becoming more and more true over time that "nothing lasts forever." The manufacturers of the latest and greatest tech gadgets rely on their loyal customers to buy the newest version year after year. In order to help motivate these future sales, they even build products with the expectation that they will become obsolete in a relatively short period of time. While I am not susceptible to tech toys, I am familiar with the temptation to purchase things simply because they're cool. One tactic to avoid many such purchases is to pause and, as vividly as possible, imagine the day that I am throwing it away.

Think of your last trip to a Goodwill or similar thrift store. Every item on that thrift store shelf was once someone's prized purchase. Those jeans were probably the height of fashion. That VCR may have been one of the most advanced pieces of home entertainment equipment available on the market. As you are contemplating a purchase, I encourage you to imagine the day that you put it in a trash bag and drag it to the curb for collection, keeping in mind that every ounce of "trash" in a landfill was once likely viewed as a "treasure." Realizing how quickly today's treasures become tomorrow's trash can save you thousands.

FINDING NORTH

In Chapter 1 of this book, we explored a technique for avoiding mistakes in life: "Working Backward from Defeat." The trick was to picture someone who has failed in an area where you wish to succeed and avoid doing the things that they did to get there. The flip side of that coin is working backward from success. Returning to our earlier example involving the decision to overeat, we can think ahead to our motivation for making good decisions. In this case, it might involve fitting into your favorite clothes, feeling attractive, or getting great feedback from your physician after your next annual physical exam. Whatever the desired outcome, you can likely picture yourself on the other side of hundreds of good decisions. In your mind, ask that person what they did to get there. They may talk about what they eat and drink, what exercises they do, or perhaps how they choose to take the stairs when faced with the option to take the elevator. Now that this future version of yourself has given you their playbook, it is up to you to simply do what they did to get there. That future version of you already knows the path. Just follow it.

When it comes to personal finances, the simplest definition of a plan is a series of steps for getting from someone's current condition to whatever condition they desire in the future. As Lewis Carroll famously wrote, "If you don't know where you are going, any road will get you there." This is to say that your first job is to give the most precise definition that you can of your desired goal. Once you know your destination, you can then start taking the necessary roads to ensure your successful arrival. In practical terms, this means asking yourself one very simple question every time that you are faced with a decision. "Which choice brings me closer to my ideal future? Which takes me farther away?" Now, your only job is to choose accordingly. If you let your goal become your "true north," your day-to-day task simply becomes following your compass to your predetermined destination.

CONCLUSION

There is abundant evidence that the ability to delay gratification has a direct link to significant achievements and well-being in multiple areas of a person's life. This is as true for a three-year-old earning an extra marshmallow as it is for a retiree living off of the returns from investments they made decades earlier. The marshmallows may get bigger, but the principle stays the same. Not everyone was fortunate enough to have had the ability to exercise such self-control as some of the three-year-olds in the Stanford Marshmallow Experiment. Fortunately, there are tools to help us master delayed gratification, even if we didn't start out with it. Visualizing the future and setting personal policies can be valuable practices. Over the longer term, designing our ideal outcomes and being accountable to ourselves for taking steps towards that future can help to produce a long series of good decisions that it will take to get there.

TOOLS FOR YOUR KIT

KEY INSIGHT: Every decision you make either builds your future or borrows against it. Success doesn't require perfection. It requires consistency, restraint, and alignment.

MENTAL REFRAME: You're not depriving your present; you're investing in your future. Saying "no" to something today is often a "yes" to the person you want to become.

PRACTICAL TOOL: Use these three practices to build long-term clarity and discipline:

1. **Future Self Exercise:**
    - Visualize your future self five years from now. Ask:
    - What did they do daily to get where they are?
    - What did they say "no" to, even when it was tempting?

2. **Personal Policies:**
    - Leave the credit card at home
    - Don't make big purchases the same day you find them
    - Use phone alarms, sticky notes, or saved photos to remind yourself of past regrets

3. **The Trash Test:**
    - Before buying something, imagine how it would feel to throw it away in 6 months.
    - If the answer is "not great," walk away.

ACTION STEP: Write one sentence that describes your ideal life. Then review a recent financial or lifestyle decision. Did it move you closer or further from that vision?

BONUS TOOL: Use your True North filter: Before you say "yes" to anything, ask if it aligns with your highest values. If it doesn't, it's not worth your time, energy, or dollars.

CHAPTER 12

CONCLUSION:

TAKING FLIGHT

Across these pages, I've shared tools and tactics for improving your life through better decisions. I've pointed out pitfalls and provided ways over or around them. We explored a few of life's biggest decisions and shared frameworks to increase your odds of success. You've seen public case studies and personal stories alike. You have the tools. Now comes a question that is as difficult as it is inevitable. "Now What?"

In the chapter on biases, we cited a well-known example of a space shuttle tragedy. Though we explored that disaster as an example of bias, space travel also offers inspiration for our own personal 'moon shots.'

> *"We choose to go to the moon in this decade and do the other things not because they are easy, but because they are hard. Because that goal will serve to organize and measure the best of our energies and skills, because that challenge is one that we're willing to accept. One we are unwilling to postpone."*
> *—John F. Kennedy*

PREVENTING CRASHES

The National Business Aviation Association (NBAA) stated in a 2017 article that "Weather is a contributing factor in 35 percent of general aviation accidents." So here's the first crash prevention tip: only fly on perfect-weather days. Can it be this simple? What if the world of air travel can't function on only the pretty days? What if people and packages still need to arrive on time, even if conditions are less than perfect? Don't some flights land safely even on days when the weather is bad? Of course they do. But accidents rarely happen from weather alone.

In the same article mentioned above, the NBAA continued to point out that in most weather-related accidents, "a failure to recognize deteriorating weather continues to be a frequent cause or contributing factor." Most accidents happen when weather combines with poor human judgment. The weather is beyond our control. The human failure to recognize risk? That's preventable. The International Council of Aircraft Owner and Pilot Associations says that "Some weather-related accidents are founded on the pilot's lack of knowledge of weather theory and/or weather services," and "Some happen because the pilot failed to obtain a good weather briefing, or to heed the warning signs they discovered in a weather briefing."

The more practical solution? Hire pilots who make better decisions in bad weather. What those quotes all point to is simple: a failure to recognize and react to danger. You can't fly as if every day is sunny and windless. This leads us back to our core topic of making better decisions.

Few flights are less forgiving than space travel. In a shuttle launch, there's no room for error. It is for this reason that many astronauts are trained through months of routine and repetition. Some even eat the exact same breakfast daily. This reduces early decision fatigue by removing a choice first thing in the morning. The second benefit of a precisely repeated structure is that anything out of the ordinary will be more likely to stand out and potentially set off some warning signals in the minds of the astronauts. Routine sharpens awareness, and anything unusual stands out more quickly. This lessens the chance of behaving like a pilot who experiences the "failure to recognize" a problem. The next question: once you recognize danger, how do you respond? The answer? Training and repetition. To answer this question, we return to training and repetition. Months of training ensure that the right response becomes automatic. There is a saying that has been adapted for use by military organizations like the Navy Seals, as well as first responders like police and firefighters. It is an altered version of the words of the Greek poet Archilochus. The modern translation is as follows:

> "Under pressure, you don't rise to the occasion,
> you sink to the level of your training."

You have been given the tools for making better decisions in your own day-to-day life. Big decisions will come. But every day offers the chance to build your training. Use your tools, even on small decisions, until they become second nature. Slowly but surely, the level of your internal training will rise, and your chances of a mishap will decline.

FEAR OF FLYING - AND LIVING

As President Franklin D. Roosevelt said, "The only thing we have to fear is fear itself." That must mean fear is something worth paying attention to. Ryan Holiday, in *The Obstacle is the Way*, reminds us: 'Blessings and burdens are not mutually exclusive.'

Often, fear is the signal that something great lies just ahead. Nelson Mandela once stated that "courage was not the absence of fear, but the triumph over it. The brave man is not he who does not feel afraid, but he who conquers that fear." Even astronauts feel fear before launch. Moving forward anyway is what makes the mission possible. Fear often means you're growing by trying something new, reaching forward, and progressing. If these things were not happening, you would likely feel nothing at all.

In many ways, I am in the business of helping people to make changes in their lives. On some level, I have always known this to be true. While it is easy to recognize the gravity of this change when you are helping someone through a huge life event like divorce or the death of a loved one, less obvious may be the discomfort of simply changing from a familiar strategy or a comfortable professional relationship. These kinds of fears are no more or less valid than that of the astronaut. They are faced with the prospect of moving away from something that is comfortable and familiar, that being the surface of the earth. The first step for the astronaut is to face her fear and get off the ground. Similarly, we must each demonstrate the courage to move beyond the old ideas that no longer serve us.

Perhaps we should occasionally seek out scary obstacles to overcome. The presence of fear may act as a guidepost along a road of personal growth. Facing our fears might not be easy, but it may be necessary to improve our lives and achieve our highest potential.

"Everything you want is on the other side of fear."
— *Jack Canfield*

LIFT OFF

And there it is, the answer to that dreaded question: "Now what?" Review the tools provided to you throughout this book. Pick the ones

100

that resonate. Practice them. Use them until they become part of how you think. You won't just know how to make better choices, but you'll be a better decision-maker.

The "biggies" will come, and they might still stop you in your tracks. Hopefully, this book included a chapter that speaks directly to your own big choices. If not, I encourage you to reread some of the concepts that you don't use every day. Perhaps tools like the PRism Protocol or a decision tree will assist you in navigating through your choices.

Your next step may not be easy, but it is simple. Take a step. That's it. That's where it starts. Sometimes, the hardest part of making a difficult decision is knowing where to start. Many of the tactics covered here can provide you with that starting point. These may be something as basic as identifying your biases, questioning your assumptions, or employing the Eisenhower Matrix. Once you have taken the first step, don't be surprised if the second and third are considerably easier. Get started, and don't be surprised when momentum takes over.

I congratulate you for having made the commitment to taking the first step towards successfully making many future decisions. By picking up this book and reading through its pages, you have undoubtedly better equipped yourself for the choices ahead. By taking this step, you do not remain standing on the launchpad but have left the ground and are already being propelled toward better outcomes in your own life.

WAYPOINTS

DECISION-MAKING FRAMEWORKS

- Use fast and slow thinking wisely.
- Build a decision tree.
- Learn from others' past "lines."

RELATIONSHIPS AND PARTNERSHIPS

- Don't burn a good ship.
- Avoid decisions made under duress.
- Use the Eisenhower Matrix.
- Work backward from disaster.
- Engineer your own miracle.

PERSONAL GEOGRAPHY & EDUCATIONAL CHOICES

- Question your assumptions.
- Key education questions: Is college right for me? Is now the right time? What careers match my strengths and lifestyle?
- Investigate your school choices thoroughly: location, cost, outcomes, and facilities.

BUSINESS & CAREER DECISIONS

- Treat yourself like a business (CEO, CMO, CFO roles).
- Build your board of directors.
- Evaluate remote vs. in-office work strategically.

FINANCIAL THINKING

- Vet your advice sources.

- Know your "real wealth."
- Thoreau's financial framework: want less or earn more; cut the unnecessary.

RISK & PROBABILITY

- Start with math (probability and expected value).
- Watch for asymmetry in risks.
- Apply the six-question risk symmetry test.

DECISION FATIGUE

- Reduce your daily decision load.
- Time your big decisions for peak mental clarity.
- Don't decide on an empty stomach.

DELAYED GRATIFICATION & FUTURE THINKING

- Talk to your future self.
- Use personal policies to pre-commit.
- Try the "trash test."
- Follow your True North.

TAKING FLIGHT – FINAL TOOLS

- Avoid poor decisions under pressure by preparing ahead.
- Respect fear; it often points to growth.
- Start. Then keep going.

ABOUT THE AUTHOR

Matt Miller is a thoughtful, analytical, and principled decision-maker who blends deep analysis and expertise with a broader humanistic understanding of how people navigate life's hardest choices. He's spent decades helping people make sense of uncertainty by combining lived experience with pattern recognition, logic with empathy.

Founder of Upleft and CERTIFIED FINANCIAL PLANNER® professional, Matt has "been there and done the math," but Waypoints isn't about spreadsheets. It's about the quiet decisions that shape the arc of a life. Whether the question is when to leave a job, how to choose a partner, or where to live next, Matt brings calm clarity to the moments that matter most.

His writing is grounded but expansive, built on the belief that good outcomes come not from having all the answers, but from asking the right questions. He serves as a guide, not because he knows your path, but because he's spent a lifetime learning how to walk his own with intention.

When he's not working with clients of his firm, Upleft, Matt shares insights through essays, interviews, and his well-regarded blog, The Logbook. Waypoints is his first book, and for many, it won't be their last encounter with his work.

Matt lives with his wife and dogs on the Olympic Peninsula of Washington State, where he helps people make sense of their finances and their futures.

APPENDIX

The following worksheets are practical applications of the decision-making frameworks discussed throughout this book. Each worksheet is designed to help you work through specific types of decisions using structured approaches that reduce bias and improve outcomes. Feel free to print or photocopy these pages for personal use.

Includes:

- Prism Sorting Sheet
- Risk Symmetry Grid
- Cognitive Bias Cheat Sheet
- Bias Spotter Checklist
- Pre-Decider Grid
- Waypoint Mapping Tool
- Future Snapshot Journal
- Decision Debrief Log

PRism Sorting Sheet

Principles

Non-negotiable values that guide who your are and how you live.

Priorities

Important areas of focus that deserve your time and energy.

Preferences

Nice-to- haves that are flexible and may change over time.

RISK SYMMETRY GRID

FILL IN YOUR OWN

	BEST-CASE SCENARIO	WORST-CASE SCENARIO
WHAT IS THE OUTCOME?		
HOW LIKELY IS IT?		
HOW WOULD IT AFFECT ME?		

How to use this Risk Symmetry Grid:

1. Describe your best- and worse-case outcomes for a decision.
2. Eliminate the likelihood of each.
3. Reflect on how each outcome would affect your life.
4. If the downside feels far worse than the upside is good, the risk may be asymmetric.

→ Adjust your strategy accordingly.

COGNITIVE BIASES CHEAT SHEET

BIAS NAME	DESCRIPTION
ANCHORING	Fixating on the first piece of info you receive
CONFIRMATION BIAS	Noticing info that supports what you already believe.
GROUPTHINK	Suppressing disagreement to maintain group harmony.
SELF-INTEREST BIAS	Allowing personal gain to influence decisions.
AFFECT HEURISTIC	Letting emotions override logical analysis.
SALIENCY BIAS	Overweighting the most noticeable info.
AVAILABILITY BIAS	Relying on recent or vivid examples.
HALO EFFECT	Allowing one positive trait to skew overall judgement.

BIAS SPOTTER CHECKLIST

BIAS	QUESTION	YES	NO
ANCHORING	Am I basing this on the first info I heard?		
CONFIRMATION BIAS	Am I ignoring info that challenges my belief?		
GROUPTHINK	Am I going along just to keep the peace?		
SELF-INTEREST BIAS	Could I be favoring an outcome that benefits me?		
AFFECT HEURISTIC	Am I being swayed by my mood or emotion?		
SALIENCY BIAS	Is something standing out just because it's loud or flashy?		
AVAILABILITY BIAS	Am I overestimating based on recent or vivid examples?		
HALO EFFECT	Am I letting one good trait color my full opinion?		

PRE-DECIDER GRID

Lock in good habits by making everyday decisions once.

RECURRING DECISION	DEFAULT CHOICE	WHY THIS WORKS

WAYPOINT MAPPING TOOL

Break down a big goal or transition into small, trackable steps. Use the space between to define key actions.

○ **WAYPOINT 1:** [   ]

STEPS TO GET THERE:

_____

_____

_____

_____

_____

○ **WAYPOINT 2:** [   ]

STEPS TO GET THERE:

_____

_____

_____

_____

_____

○ **WAYPOINT 3:** [   ]

STEPS TO GET THERE:

_____

_____

_____

_____

_____

○ **WAYPOINT 4:** [   ]

STEPS TO GET THERE:

_____

_____

_____

○ **WAYPOINT 5:** [   ]

FUTURE SNAPSHOT JOURNAL

Imagine each future path as if you're already living it. Describe your day, feelings, and tradeoff.

PATH A—"IF I CHOOSE..."

PATH B—"IF I CHOOSE..."

PATH C—"IF I CHOOSE..."

DECISION DEBRIEF LOG

Reflect on past decisions to learn what worked, what didn't, and how to improve your process.

DECISIONS I MADE	WHAT I HOPED FOR	WHAT HAPPENED	WHAT I LEARNED	WOULD I DO IT DIFFERENTLY

ACKNOWLEGEMENTS

MY GRATITUDE BEGINS AND ENDS WITH MY WIFE, AMY. Her eyes are the first to read every word I put out into the world, and often the third, fifth, and tenth as well. She is my fiercest editor, most loyal reader, and the steady presence who makes my work (and my world) possible.

To the readers who stick with me through blogs, newsletters, and long-winded LinkedIn posts, thank you. Special thanks to Terry Gallagher, Angela Kokinakos, and John Anderson, whose feedback has kept me writing when I might have otherwise stopped.

To Charlie Benson, who once suggested I might have a knack for writing: I'm still not sure you were right, but I appreciated the nudge.

I credit my parents for shaping how I communicate. Dad showed me how to create connections with language and express ideas simply and directly. From my mom, I learned to make my words count, even if it ruffles a few feathers.

To the clients of Upleft, thank you. You are the reason I put my ideas into writing in the first place. A handful of early essays from our company blog, The Logbook, sparked my deeper exploration into the art and science of decision-making. Without that, Waypoints might never have come to life.

True to my words above, my gratitude begins and ends with my bride. Thank you, Amy. I love you, and couldn't have done it without you.

BIBLIOGRAPHY

BOOKS AND ACADEMIC SOURCES:

Baumeister, Roy F., et al. "Ego Depletion: Is the Active Self a Limited Resource?" *Journal of Personality and Social Psychology*, vol. 74, no. 5, 1998, pp. 1252–1265.

Baumeister, Roy F., and John Tierney. *Willpower: Rediscovering the Greatest Human Strength.* Penguin Books, 2011.

Brokaw, Tom. *Boom!: Voices of the Sixties – Personal Reflections on the '60s and Today.* Random House, 2007.

Cuban, Mark. *How to Win at the Sport of Business: If I Can Do It, You Can Do It.* Diversion Books, 2011.

Francis-Tan, Andrew, and Hugo M. Mialon. "'A Diamond Is Forever' and Other Fairy Tales: The Relationship between Wedding Expenses and Marriage Duration." *SSRN*, 2015. HTTPS://SSRN.COM/ABSTRACT=2501480.

Galloway, Scott. *The Algebra of Happiness: Notes on the Pursuit of Success, Love, and Meaning.* Portfolio, 2019.

Gladwell, Malcolm. *Blink: The Power of Thinking Without Thinking.* Little, Brown and Company, 2005.

Heatherton, Todd F., and Dylan D. Wagner. "Cognitive Neuroscience of Self-Regulation Failure." *Trends in Cognitive Sciences*, vol. 15, no. 3, 2011, pp. 132–139.

Holiday, Ryan. *The Obstacle Is the Way: The Timeless Art of Turning Trials into Triumph.* Portfolio, 2014.

Iyengar, Sheena S., and Mark R. Lepper. "When Choice Is Demotivating: Can One Desire Too Much of a Good Thing?" *Journal of Personality and Social Psychology*, vol. 79, no. 6, 2000, pp. 995–1006.

Kahneman, Daniel. *Thinking, Fast and Slow.* Farrar, Straus and Giroux, 2011.

Kasparov, Garry. *How Life Imitates Chess: Making the Right Moves—from the Board to the Boardroom.* Bloomsbury, 2007.

Levav, Jonathan, and Shai Danziger. "Extraneous Factors in Judicial Decisions." *Proceedings of the National Academy of Sciences*, vol. 108, no. 17, 2011, pp. 6889–6892. HTTPS://DOI.ORG/10.1073/PNAS.1018033108.

Mischel, Walter, Ebbe B. Ebbesen, and Anton R. Zeiss. "Cognitive and Attentional Mechanisms in Delay of Gratification." *Journal of Personality and Social Psychology*, vol. 21, no. 2, 1972, pp. 204–218.

Newell, Allen, and Herbert A. Simon. *Human Problem Solving*. Prentice-Hall, 1972.

Roosevelt, Eleanor. *You Learn by Living: Eleven Keys for a More Fulfilling Life*. Harper Perennial, 1960.

Schwartz, Barry. *The Paradox of Choice: Why More Is Less*. Harper Perennial, 2004.

Thoreau, Henry David. *Walden*. Ticknor and Fields, 1854.

ONLINE ARTICLES AND REPORTS:

All Star Home. "Survey: Nearly Half of Americans Live in Their Hometown." *All Star Home*, Aug. 2023. HTTPS://WWW.ALLSTAR-HOME.COM/BLOG/HOMETOWN-LIVING-SURVEY.

Bureau of Economic Analysis. "Regional Price Parities." *U.S. Department of Commerce*, 2022. HTTPS://WWW.BEA.GOV/DATA/PRICES-INFLA-TION/REGIONAL-PRICE-PARITIES-STATE-AND-METRO-AREA.

Governors Highway Safety Association. "Pedestrian Traffic Fatalities by State: 2022 Preliminary Data." *GHSA*, Mar. 2023. HTTPS://WWW.GHSA.ORG/RESOURCES/PEDESTRI-ANS23.

KPA. "2024 Car Buyer Trust and Transparency Study." *KPA Services LLC*, 2024. HTTPS://WWW.KPA.IO/BLOG/KPA-STUDY-SHOWS-AUTOMOTIVE-BUYERS-WANT-MORE-TRANSPAR-ENCY.

LendingTree. "Why So Many Millennials and Gen Zers Live in Their Hometowns." *LendingTree*, Aug. 2023.

HTTPS://WWW.LENDINGTREE.COM/PERSONAL/WHY-YOUNG-ADULTS-STAY-IN-HOMETOWNS-STUDY.

National Safety Council. "Odds of Dying." *NSC Injury Facts*, 2023. HTTPS://INJURYFACTS.NSC.ORG/ALL-INJURIES/PREVENTABLE-DEATH-OVERVIEW/ODDS-OF-DYING.

NBAA. "Top 10 Weather-Related Accident Factors." *National Business Aviation Association*, 2017. HTTPS://NBAA.ORG/AIRCRAFT-OPERATIONS/SAFETY/TOP-10-WEATHER-RELATED-ACCIDENT-FACTORS.

Stanford Law School. "Three Strikes Project." *Stanford University*, 2011–2013. HTTPS://LAW.STANFORD.EDU/THREE-STRIKES-PROJECT.

SURVEYS AND DATA SETS:

Indeed. "Relocation Survey." *Indeed Career Insights*, 2022. HTTPS://WWW.INDEED.COM/LEAD/RELOCATION-JOB-SEARCH-SURVEY.

Federal Reserve. "Report on the Economic Well-Being of U.S. Households." *Board of Governors of the Federal Reserve System*, May 2023. HTTPS://WWW.FEDERALRESERVE.GOV/PUBLICATIONS/2023-ECONOMIC-WELL-BEING-OF-US-HOUSEHOLDS-IN-2022.HTM.

YOUTUBE VIDEOS:

Rosen, Eric. "My Deepest Opening Preparation in the Queen's Gambit Declined." *YouTube*, uploaded by Eric Rosen, 12 July 2021. HTTPS://WWW.YOUTUBE.COM/WATCH?V=5RND8DAC1AI.

OTHER MEDIA/VISUAL AIDS REFERENCED:

NRICH. "The Derren Brown Coin Flipping Scam." *University of Cambridge*. HTTPS://NRICH.MATHS.ORG/PROBLEMS/DERREN-BROWN-COIN-FLIPPING-SCAM.

WAYPOINTS INDEX

FTX 32
Fulghum, Robert 19

G

H

I

J

S

T

U

www.ingramcontent.com/pod-product-compliance
Lightning Source LLC
Chambersburg PA
CBHW051632120626
46551CB00014B/2048